coast

MAGAZINE

250

Weekends
by the sea

First published in Great Britain by
Simon & Schuster UK Ltd, 2011
A CBS COMPANY

Copyright © 2011 The National
Magazine Company Limited
Copyright in the photographs and
illustrations in this book belongs to
The National Magazine Company
Limited, except where otherwise
indicated (see Picture credits)
Coast Magazine is a registered trade
mark of The National Magazine
Company Limited, Hearst
Communications, Inc.

1 3 5 7 9 10 8 6 4 2

SIMON & SCHUSTER
ILLUSTRATED BOOKS
Simon & Schuster UK Ltd
222 Gray's Inn Road
London
WC1X 8HB

www.simonandschuster.co.uk

Simon & Schuster Australia
Sydney

Editorial Director: Francine Lawrence
Designer: Richard Proctor
Picture Researcher: Emma O'Neill
Production Manager: Katherine
Thornton

A CIP catalogue record for this book
is available from the British Library

ISBN 978-0-85720-273-4

Printed and bound in China

coast

M A G A Z I N E

250

Weekends
by the sea

Compiled and edited by Paula McWaters

**SIMON &
SCHUSTER**
ILLUSTRATED

London · New York · Sydney · Toronto

A CBS COMPANY

This page: Durdle Door, Dorset

Where did you spend your most memorable weekend last year? I bet it wasn't in a shopping mall or a DIY store. Weekends that stay in my memory involve a view of the sea, a stretch of beach, a tasty fish supper and a friendly B&B to return to. If you think back to your own childhood, it's likely that the days you fondly remember involve a sandy beach and the sound of the ocean, too.

There has never been a better time to visit the British seaside: hotels and B&Bs have spruced up their act, resorts are offering better attractions, the number of Blue Flag beaches has increased and there is greater access to coastal paths. Plus, a weekend in your own country means no more struggling with airports and flight cancellations.

This book has 250 suggestions for great weekends. They may include a simple stroll along a cliff path or a dip in a secret cove. They could involve a little planning, such as arranging a surfing lesson or booking tickets for a music festival. Perhaps you have a hankering for a crab sandwich or some fresh fish and chips? Or you want to know the best beach to take your dog – you will find suggestions for all these and many more here. I am sure that *250 Weekends By The Sea* will give you plenty of ideas for trips to the coast and lots of opportunities to create happy memories for the future.

Clare

Clare Gogerty, editor, coast Magazine
PS For more on what our shores have to offer, visit allaboutyou.com/coast

How to use this book

There are so many different reasons you might want to spend a weekend by the coast, whether it's to mess about in a boat, have a drink by the shore or simply feel some sand between your toes. This book will inspire you and take you there.

It is a collection of 250 of the recommendations we have made in coast Magazine: exhilarating coastal paths to walk, wide beaches to let your dog run along, good cycling routes… the list goes on.

Where we have a specific suggestion about a place to stay, we have included it. Elsewhere, we start with the 'excuse to go' (a gorgeous beach, a place to spot seals…), then recommend a location and supply local contact numbers and websites, giving you the freedom to choose your own accommodation.

Every issue of coast is filled with a wealth of ideas for great weekends by the sea. In this book we have collected 250 of them, all in one handy, keep-by-your-side or in-your-glove-compartment book. We have also included some Shore Spotter's Guides to help you know what to look for when you're down by the sea. Enjoy!

A note about dot coms

It may seem obvious, but you'll need to put www. before all the website addresses we have quoted in this book, so englishriviera.co.uk becomes www.englishriviera.co.uk. We have left them off to avoid repetition and also to save a little space for more interesting things

Weekends for...

Weekends for getting away from it all

If you're longing to leave the hubbub and hurly-burly behind you for a while, the British coast is the very best place to do it. With nothing but waves in front of you and open skies above you, it's possible to forget the stresses of daily life and soothe your soul with the mesmerising power of the ocean. A short period of escape will invigorate and inspire you, and the rhythmic, cyclical sound of the waves is therapeutic in itself. We've uncovered some great places to help you find that all-important sense of calm.

1 For northerly isolation

Balnakiel Bay, Durness, Highlands

Balnakiel Bay lies on the western edge of the neck of land leading to the rocky headland of Faraid Head. From the beach, walk the two miles to the tip jutting out into the Pentland Firth. It's about as far north as you can get on mainland Britain, with just the sound of the waves crashing thunderously on the wide white sands and the eyeless military installations perched on the hills for company. Ponder the view across the bay from the roofless and ivy-clad 17th-century Durness Old Church.

INFO Durness Tourist Information 0845 225 5121 visithighlands.com

STAY In Balnakiel or Durness 0845 225 5121 visithighlands.com

2 For escaping the crowds

Beady Pool, St Agnes, Isles of Scilly

Beady Pool on the south-eastern shore of St Agnes, the most south-westerly of the Scilly Isles, is not just 28 miles from Land's End, it is a

Balnakiel Bay, Durness, Highlands

world away in time and place. St Agnes is home to a community of 72, there is no hotel and even in summer, when daytrippers descend on the tiny island, many do not make it beyond the enticing curving sand bar between St Agnes and Gugh. So press on along the coastal footpath to Beady Pool, to search in the coarse-grained sand for glass and terracotta beads washed up from a 17th-century shipwreck, or simply to stand and stare at the Atlantic waves beating on the rocky shoreline.

INFO St Mary's Tourist Information Centre 01720 424031 simplyscilly.co.uk, or st-agnes-scilly.org

STAY On St Mary's simplyscilly.co.uk

3 For island camping

Rackwick Bay, Hoy, Orkney

Camping on a fine sand and boulder-strewn beach on the north-western 'highland' coast of Orkney's second largest island is not for the faint-hearted or overloaded, say aficionados, but the experience is magical. The stone-walled grass camp fitting 12 tents has use of a heather-thatched stone bothy: light a fire here using beach driftwood and seaweed. With no shops nearby, and no access by car, the site is bounded by 200-metre-high cliffs and steep, heathery hills. Old Man of Hoy, the famous sea stack, is a three-hour round walk. You can also camp at Rackwick Outdoor Centre, with use of hostel facilities. INFO Orkney Tourist Information 01856 872856 visitorkney.com, or visitscotland.com STAY Rackwick Bay 01856 872856 visitorkney.com. Rackwick Outdoor Centre hostelsorkney.co.uk

4 For sheltered swimming

Petit Port Bay, St Martins, Guernsey

Limited parking and a steep climb down 270 steps deters some visitors from this rocky bay. But the climb is well worth it. The cliffs shelter the bay from the wind, and its situation on the south-eastern coast of the island means it enjoys plenty of sunshine. There is lots of deep pure sand and the water is cold but clean. Warm up afterwards with a hot chocolate in the nearby brasserie and a walk to the Doyle Column, a 396-foot-high monument to Governor Sir John Doyle who died in 1834. INFO 01481 723552 visitguernsey.com STAY In St Martins or St Peter Port 01481 723552 visitguernsey.co.uk

5 For walkers

Llanbedrog, Gwynedd

At high tide, the sea laps against the boundary wall of The Boathouse, former fishermen's cottages now converted into two self-catering properties. At low tide, the sandy beach stretches for miles, as do the views to the Snowdonia mountain range. But if you want to venture further afield, the beach is also the start of a 16km walk from Llanbedrog to Chwilog, part of the new Llyn Coastal Path in North Wales, a 95-mile

Sanna Bay, Kilchoan, Highlands

route stretching from Caernarfon to Porthmadog. INFO Pwllheli Tourist Information Centre 01758 613000 visitsnowdonia.info, or walkingnorthwales.co.uk STAY The Boathouse 07930 562403 beachboathouse.com

6 For artistic reflection
Dymchurch, Kent

In 1921, the war artist Paul Nash rented a cottage at Dymchurch with his wife Margaret to recuperate from a nervous breakdown.

Left: Gateway to the sea, Outer Hebrides

Painting the sea and landscape as a series of interlocking planes and geometric shapes, for him the vast man-made sea wall designed to protect Romney Marsh from flooding became emblematic of the continuous interaction between land and 'the cold and cruel waters... pounding and rattling along the shore'. But on a gentle summer's day, the tide is altogether more benevolent, washing the beach twice daily to leave a vast expanse of sand almost a quarter of a mile wide. INFO Folkestone, Hythe &

Romney Marsh Tourist Information 01303 258594 discoverfolkestone.co.uk STAY In Dymchurch or nearby Dungeness 01303 258594 discoverfolkestone.co.uk

7 For jaw-dropping views
Sanna Bay, Kilchoan, Highlands

The west-facing side of Sanna Bay has it all: magnificent white sand beaches, fascinating rockpools, extensive sand dunes and water that varies from deep, dark blue to stunning light turquoise. But make the short climb

Llanbedrog Llyn Peninsula, Gwynedd

north to the high ground of Sanna Point and you are rewarded with views to the islands of Eigg and Rum to the north, with Skye in the distance, round to Ardnamurchan Point and its lighthouse to the south-west, with the island of Coll beyond. Due west there is nothing but sea... Unsurprisingly, this is a favoured haunt of painters and photographers.
INFO Kilchoan Tourist Information 01972 510 711, or Strontian Tourist Information 01967 402 382 visitscotland.com
STAY In Kilchoan ardnamurchan.com or undiscoveredscotland.co.uk

8 For endless space

Murlough, Dundrum, County Down

Its remote location on the north-east coast of Northern Ireland and its size make Murlough National Nature Reserve as much a haven for harassed humans as for the many rare and endangered wildlife found there. Lose yourself in the 282 hectares of sand dunes, heathland and woodland surrounded by estuary and sea, or simply take in the panoramic view over the coastline.
INFO Murlough National Nature Reserve 028 4375 1467 nationaltrust.org.uk/murlough
STAY In Dundrum or nearby Newcastle 08000 397000 discovernorthernireland.com

9 For heathland and lakes

Studland Bay, Dorset

The bucket-and-spade beach is just one of the glories of Studland Bay. Hidden behind it is a little-known area of heathland and Little Sea, a freshwater lake cut off from the sea by the dunes. Studland Heath is part of Thomas Hardy's Egdon Heath, the setting for his novel, *The Return of the Native*. Fuel up at the Knoll House Hotel, before following one of its nine local walks for, as the hotel suggests, 'What better excuse for yielding to the temptation of sponge pudding and custard than an ensuing six-mile tramp through the Dorset heathland!'
INFO 01929 422885 visitswanageandpurbeck.co.uk. The Knoll House Hotel 01929 450450

knollhouse.co.uk
STAY In Swanage or nearby Lulworth 01929 552740 visitswanageandpurbeck.co.uk

10 For blissful solitude

Porlock Bay, Bristol Channel, Somerset

Famously, Coleridge was disturbed in the process of writing his *Kubla Khan* by the 'person... from Porlock' who he blamed for his failure to complete the poem. Scholars beg to differ: fellow poet Roger McGough said, 'I think he got stuck.' But few will intrude on a walk along the mile-long marsh and shingle ridge between Hurlestone Point and Porlock Weir. Walk with your thoughts or spot the birdlife attracted to the tidal lagoon on the saltmarsh inland or look for plants such as the everlasting pea and yellow horned poppy growing miraculously among the shingle.
INFO 01643 863150 porlock.co.uk
STAY In Porlock or Selworth 01643 863150 porlock.co.uk

Right: Murlough, Dundrum, County Down

Weekends for family fun

For most of us, our happiest mental snapshots include days spent down by the sea: paddling in the shallows, mooching around rockpools with bucket in hand, building sandcastles or eating ice-cream on the prom. Even the journey there – with the inevitable tussles over who can see the sea first and cries of, 'Are we nearly there yet?' – is memorable. Whether you want to ride a rollercoaster, create a sand mermaid, watch a Punch and Judy show or take a ride on a donkey, we have the options here for maximum family entertainment.

This page: Punch and Judy – an old-time favourite

1 For sandcastles

**Blackpool Sands,
Dartmouth, Devon**
Owned and managed by the
same family since the 1950s,
this pretty pine-fringed cove
has a Blue Flag fine shingle
beach famed for its excellent
water quality and swimming.
The owners bring in sand
specifically for castle-building
and fill two giant sandpits on
the beach. They also provide
a bathing raft. Dogs are
barred in the summer, the
beach is cleaned daily and
watersports tuition is

available. The only pitfall
is that this family beach is
incredibly popular: at peak
season, try to arrive before
11am. Behind the beach
are the recently restored
19th-century sub-tropical
Blackpool Gardens, which
are open from April
to September.
INFO 01803 771800
blackpoolsands.co.uk.
Blackpool Gardens
01803 771801
STAY In Dartmouth or nearby
Brixham 01803 834224
discoverdartmouth.com

2 For paddling

**West Wittering,
Chichester, West Sussex**
This Blue Flag beach really
is the stuff of childhood
memory: seemingly the
sun always shines and the
shallow lagoons left at
low tide, on extensive
sandy flats, provide perfect
paddling pools for little ones.
Locals call it 'God's Pocket'
as it can be warm and sunny
here even when it's raining
elsewhere, largely because
it has its own microclimate,
sheltered by the Isle of Wight

The fun of the fair at Great Yarmouth, Norfolk

to the south-west and the Downs to the north. Lifeguards patrol in the summer months and they hand out free 'Child Safe/Sea Smart' identity bands for children to wear, to help prevent them getting lost.
INFO 01243 514143 westwitteringbeach.co.uk STAY In West Wittering 01243 775888 visitchichester.org, or nearby Bognor Regis 01243 823140 sussexbythesea.com

West Wittering, West Sussex

3 For all the fun of the fair
Great Yarmouth Pleasure Beach, Great Yarmouth, Norfolk
Opened in 1909, the historic park on a nine-acre seafront site continues to offer family spills and thrills. The largest and most popular of the 30 large rides is the Scenic Railway Roller Coaster built in 1932, but new kit includes the Skydrop, a pneumatic cylinder tower that shoots passengers 22 metres up in the air. For the fainter-hearted, there is plenty of children's entertainment, from a 100-year-old merry-go-round featuring

traditional painted 'gallopers' to amusement arcades, sweet shops and ice-cream parlours galore.
INFO 01493 844585 pleasure-beach.co.uk STAY In Great Yarmouth or nearby Lowestoft 01493 846346 great-yarmouth.co.uk

4 For all-round entertainment
Butlins, Bognor Regis, West Sussex
Billy Butlin opened his first British holiday camp in a former turnip field in Skegness in 1936 with 600 chalets and a rhododendron-bordered swimming pool;

and while 'Skeggy' (albeit a more contemporary version) is still an old favourite with many, the new, flagship Butlins resort is Bognor Regis. Its seven-storey Ocean Hotel entices visitors with comfortable family rooms, colour change lighting and rainfall showers plus a 670 square metre spa with interactive 'disco' singing showers, treatment rooms, a hot tub and a snow cave. Stay here for your whole weekend or book in as day guests and have the run of the sub-tropical Splash Waterworld and inclusive entertainment and children's activities. If it all gets too

much, you can always go for a stroll along Bognor Regis's sand and shingle Blue Flag beach.

INFO Bognor Regis Tourist Information 01243 823140 sussexbythesea.com
STAY Butlins 0845 070 4734 butlins.com

5 For donkey rides

Weston Beach, Weston-super-Mare, Somerset
Donkey rides are as much a Weston institution as the Grand Pier. Ron Mager's family business (and winner of a 2009 coast Award) was established in 1886, eight years before the pier was built. Daily from Easter to October, weather permitting, his home-bred donkeys will be out on the sands carrying children aged from 12 months to 14 years. The donkeys work for only about seven months of the year before retiring for a rest on a local farm. Meanwhile, there's always the Grand Pier, rebuilt after the fire of 2008.

INFO 01934 813769 westondonkeys.co.uk
STAY In Weston-super-Mare or nearby Clevedon 01934 888 800 visitsomerset.co.uk

Left: Donkey riding in Blackpool

6 For crabbing

The Pier, Walberswick, Suffolk
The rules state that nobody born before 1890 may enter the British Open Crabbing Championship held annually (usually in August) at this Suffolk coastal village. Once a thriving port trading in cheese, corn, timber and fish, today the harbour sees most activity on championship days when children of all ages cram the pier, bridges and riverbanks, each armed with a single line and bait of their choice to land the heaviest crab. In 2009 the 90-minute charity

Crabbing at Walberswick, Suffolk

21

championship attracted 1,252 entrants and the winning crab weighed in at 4⅝oz.

INFO Southwold Tourist Information Centre 01502 724729 visit-sunrisecoast.co.uk STAY In Walberswick or nearby Southwold 01502 724729 visit-sunrisecoast.co.uk

7 For traditional Punch and Judy

Llandudno Promenade, Llandudno, Conwy
Richard Codman, a showman from Norwich, first set up his puppet theatre tent on Llandudno's wide promenade in 1860, acting out the violent adventures of the Wooden Headed Follies with a set of figures he'd carved from driftwood found on the beach. Victorians flocking by rail to Wales's largest resort loved it, and today the Codman family continue to delight their young audiences with the exploits of the hunchback Mr Punch and his poor wife Judy. Daily Easter to mid-September at 2pm and 4pm, and 12 noon on Bank Holidays and at peak times, weather permitting.
INFO 01492 577577 visitllandudno.org.uk STAY In Llandudno or nearby Conwy 01492 577577 visitllandudno.org.uk

8 For picnics

Trebetherick, Wadebridge, Cornwall
The poet John Betjeman (1906–1984) is synonymous with this part of the north Cornish coast, specifically Trebetherick, where he spent childhood summers. His poem of the same name contains the definitive line on beach picnics: 'Sand in the sandwiches, wasps in the tea,' so what better place to lay out your rug than on the 'springy turf' of Trebetherick Point, a rocky, windswept cliff

Splashing about in the shallows

A family picnic in Norfolk

outcrop overlooking Daymer Bay. Like Betjeman you can watch the waves crashing on the remains of shipwrecks caught on the jagged rocks below or explore Greenaway, the stretch of coast with a small beach between Trebetherick Point and Hayle Bay.

INFO Padstow Tourist Information 01841 533449 padstowlive.com, or trebetherick.org

STAY In Wadebridge or nearby Padstow 01841 533449 padstowlive.com, or 01872 322900 visitcornwall.com

9 For ice-cream
Allonby, Maryport, Cumbria

A long sandy beach; views across the Solway Estuary towards southern Scotland and inland to the hills of the Lake District; windsurfing on tap; a fascinating history as a herring fishing port and sea-bathing resort… The list goes on. But the real attraction of Allonby is Twentyman's, at West End Stores, the local shop selling home-made ice-cream and old-fashioned sweets. Founded in 1920, the family firm sells 40 different ice-cream flavours made on the premises, along with 25 different kinds of topping, from cinder toffee and marshmallow to apple crumble and coconut – or go for the Allonby Whopper, a mega cornet loaded with three giant scoops.

INFO Twentyman's 01900 881247

STAY In Allonby or nearby Maryport 01900 811450 (Maryport Tourist Information) golakes.co.uk

10 For variety
Saundersfoot, Pembrokeshire

There's something for everyone at this west Wales resort. Amroth is a small village with parking along the seafront. Nearby Saundersfoot's main Blue Flag beach is good for swimming and recreation. The quiet Glen Beach can be accessed via the harbour; dogs can be walked at the north end of Saundersfoot, to Wisemans Bridge.

Retail therapy is on hand in Saundersfoot, along with a range of accommodation and restaurants serving local produce, not least St Brides Spa Hotel, perched high on the clifftop, which was voted best UK Shoreline Hotel in the 2010 coast Awards. INFO 01834 813672 visitpembrokeshire.com STAY At St Brides Spa Hotel 01834 812304 stbridesspahotel.com, or elsewhere in Saundersfoot 01834 813672 visitpembrokeshire.com

11 For meeting a penguin

Living Coasts, Torquay, Devon

There's no substitute for seeing wildlife in the wild but Living Coasts, the first and only coastal zoo in the UK, offers the guarantee of seeing sea life up close, whatever the weather conditions or the time of year. Its habitats – a seabird cliff, a seal cove, a penguin beach and a waders estuary – have been created to mimic the real thing and there is an indoor zone featuring local creatures, from spiny starfish to seahorses. It has one of the largest netted aviaries in Europe, with birds flying free over your head, while underground you can press your nose to the glass and watch seals and penguins as they swim. Open every day, except 25 December. INFO 01803 202470 livingcoasts.org.uk STAY In Torquay or in nearby Babbacombe 01803 211211 englishriviera.co.uk

12 For hostelling

Old Lifeboat House, Port Eynon, Gower

The Youth Hostel Association of England and Wales has yielded to consumer demand for a bit more privacy in recent years and undertaken wholesale modernisation of many of its hostels including this one, in a former lifeboat house at Port Eynon. The family rooms may not boast carpet, TV and Wi-Fi but they do have a washbasin and two pairs of stout bunkbeds with bedding supplied and you'll be charmed by the sound of the ebbing tide within earshot and a sandy beach within a few seconds' reach. Head east for a gentle stroll from beach to beach or west for dramatic terrain – a curving headland leading to limestone cliffs and vertiginous views. Port Eynon's hostel may not feather-bed you, but it does keep the British coastal experience thrillingly real. INFO Youth Hostel Association 0800 0191700 or 01629 592700 yha.org. Mumbles Tourist Information Centre 01792 361302 mumblesinfo.org.uk STAY Old Lifeboat House (youth hostel) 0845 371 9135 yha.org

Right: Castles in the sand

Weekends for beachcombing

Fossicking along the shore is a quintessentially British pastime and with every beach being replenished twice a day by the incoming tide, each stone unturned can reveal marine flora and fauna. Search along the shoreline and you may soon unearth fossils that are literally millions of years old. Peep into a rockpool and you enter another world, one brimming with sea creatures, from crabs and anemones to starfish and sea slugs. Just keep an eye on the tides and take care not to damage or unduly disturb marine life, as you go.

This page: Exploring the shore

Beachcombing in the Isle of Wight

1 For marine rangers
Goodrington Sands, Paignton, Devon

Children can quiz the Torbay Coast and Countryside Trust rangers about their rockpooling finds at The Seashore Centre (open every day from April to September) located on the edge of this sandy beach. The centre has seawater tanks full of local marine wildlife, interactive seashore displays and a video microscope for examining treasures, plus a Geopark room dedicated to the seas of the past. Throughout the summer, it hosts events from fossil hunts to rockpool rambles and seashore safaris, on which you can discover the weird and wonderful animals that live on our shoreline – look out for devil crabs, sea hares and worm pipefish.

INFO The Seashore Centre 01803 528841 countryside-trust.org.uk STAY In Goodrington Sands or nearby Brixham 0844 474 2233 englishriviera.co.uk

2 For crabs and sea lemons
Roome Bay, Crail, Fife

You may find shore, hermit and broad-clawed porcelain crabs as well as the occasional spider crab scuttling in the sandy-bottomed pools of this quiet, south-facing bay. Butterfish, blennies and brown fish abound and the odd pipefish, a relative of the seahorse, also washes up. Summer rockpoolers may even find sea lemons (a colourful sea slug). It's worth checking out the old swimming pool lying at one end of the beach, too, as it is now colonised by sea life.

INFO Fife Beaches & Coast Officer 08451 551166 fifedirect.org.uk STAY In Crail or nearby Pittenweem 01333 450869 or 01334 472021 visitscotland.com

3 For celeb spotting
Bracelet Bay, Mumbles, Gower

This small, rocky bay next to Mumbles Lighthouse on the southern tip of Swansea Bay is a site of registered geological interest, rich in sea life. The sand-and-pebble beach harbours many limestone pools where butterfish, lightbulb sea squirts, worm pipefish and Risso's crab can be spotted. Just make sure you watch the tides. Mumbles, the village made famous by the poet Dylan Thomas, is also a site of registered celeb spotting: Hollywood actress Catherine Zeta-Jones grew up in the village and has a house there. Perhaps she and her children are keen rockpoolers?

INFO 01792 361302
visitmumbles.co.uk

STAY In Mumbles or nearby Bishopston 01792 361302 visitmumbles.co.uk

4 For catching lunch
Bembridge Ledges,
Bembridge, Isle of Wight

At low tide, the rockpools and lagoons that form on the rocky shelves stretching around the easternmost coast of the island teem with a variety of marine life, including periwinkles and crabs, so it's an ideal spot for an extended ramble. Fish are plentiful: go angling from the rocks at low tide for bass, pout, ling, bream, dogfish, pollock and ray. But to catch the reputedly very tasty local Bembridge prawn, all you need is a net and a bucket. The beachside Cabin Café sells the requisite equipment and will also lend you their pocket seashore guide to help you identify your catch.

INFO IoW Tourist Information 01983 813813 islandbreaks.co.uk. The Cabin Café 01983 875120 thecabincafe.com

STAY In Bembridge or nearby Seaview 01983 813813 islandbreaks.co.uk

5 For tide and time
South Landing,
Bridlington, Yorkshire

At the foot of the iconic white chalk cliffs of Flamborough Head, barnacles cling to the rocks as the North Sea tide ebbs away and sea creatures hide in the huge rockpools left on the pebble beach. Look out for neat, cylindrical holes in the chalk pebbles made by piddocks, bivalve molluscs similar to mussels, which live on the lower shore. Man has left his mark, too: a hand-carved timber

Rockpool discovery, Tunnels Beaches, Ilfracombe , Devon

waymark next to the Lifeboat Station depicts a fisherman, and, at low tide, the line of the medieval harbour is visible.

INFO 01262 673474 realyorkshire.co.uk

STAY In Bridlington or nearby Sewerby 01262 673474 realyorkshire.co.uk

6 For indoor rockpools

The Coastal Zone, Portrush, County Antrim

The Zone is famous for the ancient ammonite fossils embedded in the baked shale of this National Nature Reserve. If you have little ones who are keen to meet some of today's inhabitants of the many tidal pools dotted along this rocky coast, take them inside the Countryside Centre where a low-level indoor rockpool 'touch tank' allows them to get up close and personal. There are fish tanks, colouring books and an ocean-themed library, too, and if all else fails, children will love the widescreen television playing sea footage.

INFO The Coastal Zone 028 7082 3600

ni-environment.gov.uk

STAY In Portrush or nearby Portstewart 028 7082 3333 discovernorthernireland.com

7 For sunset searches

Hope Gap, Seaford, East Sussex

This beach scarcely exists at high tide but on a low tide at sunset the chalky-white rockpools reflect the colours of the dying sun. Aesthetics aside, the chalk cliffs and foreshore form a complex marine environment that dates from the Late Cretaceous period, 89–86 million years ago, and continues to erode constantly today. Take the three flights of concrete steps leading down from Seaford Head to see some very pretty beadlet anemones and speckled strawberry anemones in the rockpools. Watch out for the nasty nip of the red-eyed velvet swimming crabs if you attempt to take anything more than a photo.

INFO 01323 870280 sevensisters.org.uk

STAY In Seaford or nearby Alfriston 01323 897426 enjoysussex.info

8 For fossil foraging

Charmouth, Dorset

Charmouth, between Lyme Regis and Bridport, is said by those in the know to be one of the best locations along the 95-mile Jurassic Coast World Heritage site for discovering fossils. Join one of the guided walks run by experts from the Charmouth Heritage Coast Centre who will reveal the secrets of finding all things Jurassic, including ammonites and belemnites aplenty, plus crinoids and ichthyosaur bones. Then scamper about on your own, in search of your own treasures in and among the small pebbles on the beach, giving the foot of the cliffs a wide berth and keeping an eye on the tide. Booking is essential in the summer months for the guided walks and you'll need footwear with a firm tread.

INFO Heritage Coast Centre 01297 560772 charmouth.org, or jurassiccoast.com

STAY In Charmouth or nearby Lyme Regis 01297 442138 westdorset.com, or charmouth.org

Right: Gathering finds for closer inspection

9 For walks on the seabed

La Rocque, Jersey, Channel Islands

As the tide slips away from the sandy bars between La Rocque and Gorey Harbour on the south-east coast of the island, a vast lunar landscape emerges. Jersey Walk Adventures lead so-called 'moonwalks' to explore the gullies and reefs of this rocky inter-tidal zone. Most exciting is the night-time expedition to search for signs of tiny star-like luminescent marine life that has to survive the extremes of water pressure and being marooned high and dry for hours on end. Guided walks are advisable, as you must take very great care not to be cut off by rising tides (which can be up to 12 metres deep) and treacherous currents.

INFO Jersey Walk Adventures 01534 853138 jerseywalkadventures.co.uk

STAY In Gorey or nearby St Helier 01534 448800 jersey.com

10 For plentiful pools

Tunnels Beaches, Ilfracombe, Devon

Four hand-carved tunnels lead to secluded beaches and a tidal swimming pool where Victorian holidaymakers once sported. But the area was also a draw for biologists: after visiting Ilfracombe in 1825, Philip Henry Gosse, a friend of Charles Darwin, was inspired to write *A Naturalist's Rambles on the Devonshire Coast*, the book that sparked

Rockpool starfish find in Mumbles, Gower

a craze for marine biology across Great Britain. Today, the huge tidal range allows access to rare sea corals on very low tides, and common species are generally plentiful and easily accessible in the shallow waters. View tide times on the Tunnels Beaches website. And check out the rockpools at appropriately named Rockham Bay in nearby Woolacombe, too.

INFO 01271 879882 tunnelsbeaches.co.uk/rockpooling
STAY In Ilfracombe or nearby Combe Martin 01271 863001 visitilfracombe.co.uk

11 For seashore safaris
Botany Bay, Broadstairs, Kent

Botany Bay is so named because local smugglers were deported in a convict ship to Botany Bay in Australia. Now it is the home of a number of events run by the Thanet Coast Project. Seashore safaris reveal 'what lurks between the tides'. Youngsters love finding the edible crabs, known locally as punga crabs, and the cuttlefish eggs that look like a bunch of black grapes. Rock Doc walks are two-hour walks on other local beaches for 14+ age groups, which teach 'the language of the rocks, chalk cliffs, flints and fossils' and take you through 80 million years of history around the Thanet coast.

INFO Thanet Coast Project 01843 577672 thanetcoast.org.uk
STAY In Broadstairs or nearby Margate 01843 577577 visitthanet.co.uk

12 For shark's teeth
Walton-on-the-Naze, Essex

Shark's teeth are what you are looking for here: the bluish-grey London clay and red crag found in the cliffs and along the beach at Walton-on-the-Naze are rich hunting grounds for marine fossils, some of which notch up an exciting 53.7 million years of history. It's one of the top sites in Britain for interesting finds, so well worth an afternoon's foraging on your hands and knees through the shingle. Fossilised crabs, lobsters, dog cockles, left-handed whelks and even the occasional turtle are unearthed here and you can check out any finds on the online museum pages on naturalists Mike and Sue Cranstone-Todd's website. Known as 'the Nazeman and Nazewoman', Mike and Sue offer guided fossiling days and are a fund of information and encouragement.

INFO Walton-on-the-naze.com. Nazeman and Nazewoman 07732 986688 nazeman.fsnet.co.uk
STAY In Walton-on-the-Naze or nearby Clacton-on-Sea 01255 675542 or 01255 686633 essex-sunshine-coast.org.uk

Sea anemones

These eye-catching, jewel-like creatures may look like flowers of the sea but their attractive appearance masks their real nature: they are actually armed and dangerous to know, so

Dahlia
Urticina felina
DISTINGUISHING MARKS
A stunning, substantial anemone (up to 20cm) with bulbed tentacles of concentric reds, whites and other colours. It is usually hidden in sand and gravel when the tide is out.
WHERE TO SPOT At the base of gullies on rocky shores.
A CURIOUS THING The dahlia is a powerful predator that can catch and devour shrimps and small fish.

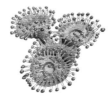

Jewel
Corynactis viridis
DISTINGUISHING MARKS Pretty and vibrantly coloured with translucent tentacles, this anemone is found in a range of different colours. Individually, it is only 2cm across, but it clumps with others in large numbers.
WHERE TO SPOT Usually found beneath the waves, it makes an exciting find at low tide in shaded rocky gullies and overhangs on exposed rocky coasts.
A CURIOUS THING It can reproduce by splitting into carbon copies, so colonies are often a carpet of the same bright colour.

Strawberry
Actinia fragacea
DISTINGUISHING MARKS Very similar to the beadlet, with pale greenish spots, but often much larger (up to 12cm).
WHERE TO SPOT On shoreline rocks, though usually a little deeper than the beadlet's stamping ground.
A CURIOUS THING Less common than the beadlet anemone, they are an important indicator of climate change.

look but don't touch. Found on rocky shores – both in and out of rockpools – these sedentary, soft-bodied animals have waving tentacles that are triggered by touch to sting and capture passing prey. On bare human skin this sting can cause a mild or strong reaction. Take a tentative peek into their watery world and see which of these fascinating creatures you can find.

Snakelocks

Anemonia viridis

DISTINGUISHING MARKS
A mass of bright green tentacles with purple tips, which are permanently exposed. Up to 20cm across.

WHERE TO SPOT On the seabed, in rockpools and attached to large seaweeds. It is widespread, but less numerous on eastern UK coasts.

A CURIOUS THING A small spider crab often lives among this anemone's barbed tentacles, which can cause a rash on human skin.

Beadlet

Actinia equina

DISTINGUISHING MARKS The familiar red, sometimes green, 'blob' found on the shore, which opens to a tentacled flower rimmed in blue in moving water. Up to 5cm across.

WHERE TO SPOT Stuck on rocks in the middle of the shore, all around the UK.

A CURIOUS THING In confined spaces, individuals actually fight each other over territory.

Plumose

Metridium senile

DISTINGUISHING MARKS This ivory-white, tall anemone (up to 30cm) has feathery tentacles when under water, but becomes a contracted, floppy blob if exposed by the tide.

WHERE TO SPOT On some pier legs and jetties, but usually in deeper water.

A CURIOUS THING They often attach themselves to shipwrecks on the seabed.

Weekends
for romance

A bracing walk along a fabulous beach, with sand between your toes, wind in your hair and salt on your lips – a weekend by the sea could be all you need to add a little magic to your love life. Take some time to spend a day or two together paddling or climbing over the rocks. Skim a few pebbles, collect a few shells or daydream at estate agents' windows before checking out that little seafood restaurant. Providing you take clothes for all weathers, a British seaside weekend can add a bit of sunshine to any relationship.

This page: Walking by the sea, Cornwall

1 For a stunning location

Knockinaam Lodge, Portpatrick, Dumfries & Galloway

This exquisite, small, country-house hotel is a tranquil hideaway, sitting at the end of a single-track lane behind its own private sandy cove on the westernmost edge of southern Scotland. There are lovely walks to be had right from the door, including a clifftop walk that traces the coastline towards the picturesque fishing town of Portpatrick. It's a great way to work up an appetite for dinner. Chef Tony Pierce holds a Michelin star for creative but unpretentious French-influenced cooking, while owner David Ibbotson is on hand to guide you through his wine cellar and whisky collection.
INFO 01776 810471
knockinaamlodge.com
STAY As above, or elsewhere in Portpatrick or Stranraer 01776 702595
visitdumfriesandgalloway. co.uk

2 For period romance

Charlestown, Cornwall

Such is the feeling of stepping back in time in this harbour village near St Austell, it's little wonder it has been the setting for period dramas including *Moll Flanders*, *The Onedin Line*, *Poldark* and the *Hornblower* series. In fact, it's so often used as a location, locals talk of having to queue behind costumed buccaneers in the village pub. There's often a tall ship in the Grade II listed Georgian harbour, which adds to the feeling of romance and history, and to the east and west of the harbour are sand and pebble beaches where tall ships often sail by. Tuck yourselves away in the comfortable Apple Store (self-catering), a wing of a grand Georgian house on the quay, and venture out for long walks up and over the cliffs to

Historic harbour, Charlestown, Cornwall

Clifftops near Godrevy, Gwithian, Cornwall

Gribben Head where the views are spectacular. Take a kite and watch it fly.
INFO 01872 322900 visitcornwall.com
STAY Apple Store 07967 104 131 antoniaspearls. co.uk, or elsewhere in Charlestown 01872 322900 visitcornwall.com

3 For running free
Gwithian, Cornwall
Kicking off your shoes and running along Gwithian Sands has to be one of the most romantic activities in coastal Britain. Not far out to sea is one of Cornwall's best known lighthouses, Godrevy Lighthouse, which inspired Virginia Woolf's *To the Lighthouse* and there's a fair chance you'll see seals and possibly dolphins. The point and beach here are owned by the National Trust. Gwithian itself is a peaceful little village just inland, backing onto sand dunes. Once you've worked up an appetite, stop at Gwithian Towans for tea, cake and one of the best views in the country or a sundowner at the licensed Sunset Surf Shop and Café: 'there's nothing but a few palm trees and the sea between us and the stunning Gwithian sunsets'.
INFO 01736 752575 sunsetsurfshop.co.uk. 01736 779190 jampotcafe.co.uk
STAY In Hayle or St Ives 01872 322900 visitcornwall.com

Osborne House, East Cowes, Isle of Wight

4 For right royal romance

East Cowes, Isle of Wight

Mrs Brown, with Judi Dench and Billy Connolly, was set in and around Osborne House, the monarch's island retreat in East Cowes. The hint of repressed emotion combined with steadfast devotion, glorious costumes and a stirling cast of British actors made for a heady mix, which still has resonance in this opulent royal pile. Now managed by English Heritage it has glorious gardens where Victoria and her beloved Albert would have enjoyed strolling à deux. It also has its own beach – a sweeping arc of sand and pebbles with mainland views. Whether you're brave enough to run naked into the sea, as Connolly did in *Mrs Brown,* is up to you. The Hambrough in Ventnor is a stylish boutique hotel with Michelin-starred food.

INFO Osborne House 01983 200022 english-heritage. org.uk/osborne. IoW Tourist Information 01983 813813 islandbreaks.co.uk

STAY The Hambrough 01983 856333 thehambrough.com, or elsewhere on the island 01983 813813 islandbreaks.co.uk

5 For a trip to Wonderland

La Rosa Hotel, Whitby, Yorkshire

Number 5 East Terrace is where Lewis Carroll used to stay on his visits to Whitby and now it has become La Rosa Hotel, a quirky whirlwind of romance and eccentricity – a tongue-in-cheek homage to his colourful Victorian idiosyncrasy. The owners have filled it with vintage furniture, nautical artefacts and Victorian curiosities, and created a veritable Wonderland for their guests. The 11 rooms all have a different theme: 'La Rosa' is sumptuously romantic,

Right: La Rosa Hotel, Whitby

Paddling in the shallows, Kent

dark wooden furniture and bindi motifs on the walls – display a passionate love for décor and design that most bigger hotels would struggle to match. Hearts will soar in the North by North West restaurant, too, where head chef John Moir's take on Highland cuisine – Loch Ewe langoustine with cantaloupe melon, hand-dived scallops – can be outshone by the sight of otters and seals by the shoreline.
INFO 0845 2255121 visitscotland.com
STAY 01445 781272 pool-house.co.uk, or stay nearby and come here for a meal

with French boudoir furniture and silk curtains; 'Little Red' is seductive; and 'Lewis' has the best sea view and a brass telescope. The beds are super-comfy with top-notch bespoke mattresses and top quality bedding, and guests love the antique baths. Breakfast is a 'picnic in bed' hamper left outside your room, containing an assortment of home-made goodies.
INFO Whitby Tourist Information 01723 383636 discoveryorkshirecoast.com

STAY La Rosa Hotel 01947 606981 larosa.co.uk or elsewhere in Whitby

6 For a natural high
Pool House, Poolewe, Wester Ross
Situated beside a loch on Scotland's west coast, and with views of the subtropical gardens at Inverewe and the mountainous Highlands, this intimate seven-room escape is surely one of the most romantic spots in Britain. Even its Eastern-inspired interiors – hand-carved doors, ornate

7 For sensuality
Seaham Hall & Serenity Spa, Seaham, Co Durham
A short walk from the North Sea coast, Seaham Hall is very well positioned. But it's not just the location that has made this manor house the north-east's premier hotel. There's the blend of history – Lord Byron married here in 1815 – and ultra-modern facilities that make it a great place to get away together. Guests are given a demo of how to use the gadgets in

their room, and the spa comes with more pools and Zen relaxation zones than a Dubai seven-star. Rooms are cool but still cosy and the restaurant offers excellent dining. And if you can tear yourselves away from all this, you can go and tramp the ancient stones of Hadrian's Wall nearby.

INFO 0191 586 4450
thisisdurham.com
STAY Seaham Hall & Serenity Spa 0191 516 1400
seaham-hall.co.uk

8 For simple pleasures

The Shack, near Cowes, Isle of Wight

If you're after a nostalgic trip, then the two-bedroom Shack will be your dream holiday home. Seemingly situated in the middle of nowhere 'in its own Dingley Dell' – but actually within seconds of sandy shores – this extended beach hut offers simple, back-to-nature living. All the power comes from either gas canisters or solar panels, and entertainment relies entirely on the occupants. The vibe is funky retro – it's charmingly stocked with vintage paraphernalia, eclectic furniture, an old Union Jack masquerading as a curtain and splashes of colour to enhance the beach house feel. Although it sleeps four everything is on a fairly dinky, beach chalet scale so with two, you'll have room to stretch out.

INFO IoW Tourist Information 01983 813813
islandbreaks.co.uk
STAY The Shack
07802 758113
vintagevacations.co.uk

9 For sand between your toes

Rye Bay Beach House, Camber Sands, East Sussex

Opening out onto Camber Sands, Rye Bay Beach House gets it right in so many ways. If you're after sustainability and good design, one look at the cedar shingles and solar tubes of this eco-friendly home will please your soul. Step in and you'll be soothed by the spacious rooms, retro interiors and luxurious touches, making it the ideal romantic getaway. Food essentials are provided and a personalised shop can be ready for your arrival. All you need to decide is whether to stand and study the dunescape from the decked balcony or walk along the sand.

INFO Rye Tourist Information 01797 229049
visitrye.co.uk, or
camber.east-sussex.co.uk
STAY Rye Bay Beach House
07961 377365
ryebaybeachhouse.com

10 For rugged good looks

Ards Peninsula, County Down

If otherworldliness is what you crave, the Ards Peninsula is where you'll find it. Dominated by the vast Strangford Lough, a haven for wading birds in their tens of thousands, it is also a prime roost for artists and designers, all drawn to its rugged beauty and clear light. The area's out-of-time spirit is attuned to windmills and Celtic forts, and its microclimate allows rare flora to flourish. At Mount Stewart you can stroll through stunning, exotic gardens and marvel at the 18th century Temple of the Winds, a Greek revival masterpiece in miniature. No wonder many brides choose it as the perfect wedding venue. And in the evening you can return to the Portaferry Hotel on the waterfront, which punches way above its three stars. Room 11 boasts a carved four-poster bed.

INFO Strangford Lough 028 4278 7823 strangfordlough.org, or nationaltrust.org.uk
STAY Portaferry Hotel 028 4272 8231 portaferryhotel.com, or elsewhere in Portaferry or Strangford 028 4272 9882 (Easter–August) or 028 9182 6846 discovernorthernireland.com

11 For retro chic
Escape, Llandudno, Conwy

Llandudno, on the North Wales coast, may sound like the sort of place your grandparents went to, but it is on the brink of a revival. The North Shore promenade offers old-fashioned attractions, as does the James Bond-like cable car to the Great Orme headland. The stylish Escape B&B is representative of its more up-to-date charms. Its nine rooms have been individually designed – styles range from 1960s retro cool to Italian inspired – so pick your mood. Each comes equipped with Blu-ray DVD players, Wi-Fi and PlayStations. Vegetarians, as well as carnivorous lovers of the Full Welsh, are catered for at breakfast, too.

INFO 01492 577577 visitllandudno.org.uk
STAY 01492 877776 escapebandb.co.uk

12 For breakfast in bed
Nineteen, Brighton, East Sussex

Ideally placed for a stay in this iconic weekend-away spot, eight-room townhouse Nineteen is a great deal more than a B&B and offers a lot more than many hotels. The rooms are more Hoxton than Hove – beds in the King rooms, for example, incorporate light installations. There's a concierge service that can fix you up with everything from theatre tickets to a recommendation for a nightclub and if you ask them, they'll fill your room with flowers and/or some champagne for the price it costs them plus VAT (with no hidden mark-ups). You can lounge about in the morning and enjoy breakfast in bed served on a white linen covered tray and at weekends they serve it with a glass of champagne or a Bloody Mary.

INFO 0300 300 0088 visitbrighton.com
STAY Nineteen 01273 675529 hotelnineteen.co.uk

Right: Room for two

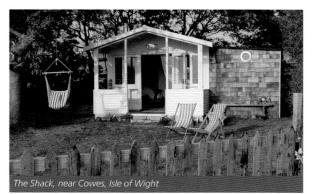

The Shack, near Cowes, Isle of Wight

Weekends for walking

There are few things as energising as breaking away from the daily grind and going for a good long walk by the sea. It's not only one of the very best forms of exercise, it can also lead you to views you just couldn't glimpse from a car. Walks can take you along rocky trails and across heathland, up to jaw-droppingly high clifftop paths and down to soft sandy beaches. So dust off those walking boots, pull on a rucksack and head for a coastal path – the going can be as tough or as gentle as you choose.

This page: The South Downs, East Sussex

1 For flourishing nature

Caerlaverock, Dumfries
(6 miles/3 hours)

This wonderful round walk to Caerlaverock Castle finishes in a hide at Caerlaverock Wildfowl and Wetland Trust. Once seen, the massed flight of the barnacle geese at dusk is never forgotten. They were hunted almost to extinction on the Solway merses, or marshes, by the mid-20th century; since then, the establishment of the Trust and the nature reserve has seen numbers boom. Look out for Caerlaverock Castle, a grim and fascinating stronghold with a bloody history. Inside the walls stands the picturesque ruin of a 17th century gentleman's residence. There is a self-catering farmhouse on the Wildfowl and Wetland Trust site or head to the lovely Cavens hotel in Kirkbean, about half an hour's drive away.
ROUTE From the WWT Centre, take the road to the shore; along floodbank for a mile; inland through Castle Wood to the castle; up

Caerlaverock, Dumfries

Ward Law Hill; back down, then on to WWT Centre via Blackshaw.
MAPS OS Explorer 314, Landranger 84 and 85
INFO Caerlaverock Wildfowl and Wetland Trust 01387 770200 wwt.org.uk/visit/caerlaverock
STAY At Cavens 01387 880234 cavens.com, or elsewhere in Dumfries 01387 253862 visitdumfriesandgalloway.co.uk

2 For organic produce

Aberaeron, Aberarth and Llanerchaeron, Ceredigion
(7 miles/4 hours*)

Shore paths lead you from Aberaeron with its beautiful Regency buildings to the beach at Aberarth, then inland through hilly country to the National Trust estate and organic farm at Llanerchaeron. Apart from restoring the lovely 18th century John Nash house, the National Trust runs Home Farm here as a working organic farm. The shop sells pork, beef and lamb from the estate, and veg and herbs from the walled garden. There's a great view from up on the hill beside Llanddewi church, taking in the coast and hills. Base yourself at the cosy Harbourmaster Hotel in Aberaeron. (*Plus time at Aberaeron.)
ROUTE From Aberaeron Harbour, take the coast path east to Aberarth, then go uphill to Llanddewi church. Take lanes to Llanerchaeron and the railway footpath back to Aberaeron.
MAPS OS Explorer 198, Landranger 146

INFO Aberaeron Tourist Information 01545 570602, or 01239 613230 tourism.ceredigion.gov.uk. Home Farm 01545 570200 nationaltrust.org.uk
STAY At Harbourmaster Hotel 01545 570755 harbour-master.com, or elsewhere in Aberaeron 01545 570602 visitaberaeron.co.uk

3 For solar-charged travel

Chichester Harbour, West Sussex (11 miles/4 hours)
This circuit of the shoreline and cornfields of Chichester Harbour is packed with wild birds. Views are wide and breezy and there's a stunning beach halfway round where you can stop for a paddle. To preview your walk from the water, or savour it in retrospect, you can take a boat trip from Itchenor jetty on Chichester Harbour Conservancy's solar-powered boat *Solar Heritage*. She also sails from Emsworth, as does Victorian oyster smack *Terror*. Look out for West Wittering's superb three-mile-long Blue Flag beach, the best one in Sussex. Nunnington Farm campsite makes a good base.

ROUTE From West Itchenor, walk 3½ miles to East Head; along West Wittering Beach for 1½ miles; up Jolliffe Road past Webb's Farm over Elms Lane, then B2179; by Redlands and Sheepwash Lane to Itchenor.
MAPS OS Explorer 120, Landranger 197
INFO 01243 775888, visitchichester.org. West Wittering Beach 01243 514143 westwitteringbeach.co.uk
STAY Nunnington Farm campsite 01243 514013 camping-in-sussex.com, or elsewhere in West Wittering 01243 775888 visitchichester.org

4 For a tiny carbon footprint

Floating Harbour, Bristol, Somerset (3 miles/half a day)
Bristol's Floating Harbour testifies to the engineering genius of Isambard Kingdom Brunel with his steamship SS *Great Britain*, the sluice system he designed and his Clifton Suspension Bridge. You can reduce your transport footprint by arriving by train or even water taxi. Look out for the Create Centre in its former warehouse on Smeaton Road above Cumberland Basin, a powerhouse of hands-on green ideas,

Floating Harbour, Bristol, Somerset

exploration and fun for children and adults.

ROUTE From SS *Great Britain*, walk clockwise around Floating Harbour.

MAPS OS Explorer 155, Landranger 172

INFO 0333 321 0101 visitbristol.co.uk. Create Centre 0117 925 0505 createbristol.org

STAY Hotel Du Vin 0117 925 5577 hotelduvin.com, or elsewhere in Bristol 0333 321 0101 visitbristol.co.uk

5 For nesting seabirds

Flamborough and Bempton Cliffs, East Yorkshire (11 miles/5 hours)

Along these dizzying cliffs, intrepid professional egg gatherers once swung in harnesses collecting seabird eggs from the cliff faces by the sackful. Now, happily, the fulmars, kittiwakes, guillemots, puffins and razorbills nest under protection each spring – more that 200,000 at Bempton Cliffs RSPB nature reserve alone. Base yourself at the cosy Crab Pot Cottage guest house in Flamborough and look out for the

poignant memorial at Flamborough's crossroads to the heroic crew of the fishing boat *Two Brothers* who drowned in the early 1900s trying to rescue colleagues in distress.

ROUTE From Flamborough, go south over Beacon Hill to the coast path; then go anti-clockwise round Flamborough Head to North Landing and on to Bempton Cliffs. Back to North Cliff; then take footpath south into Flamborough.

MAP OS Explorer 301, Landranger 101

INFO Bridlington Tourist Information 01262 673474 realyorkshire.co.uk

STAY Crab Pot Cottage B&B 01262 850555 crabpotguesthouse.co.uk, or elsewhere in Flamborough or nearby Bridlington 01262 673474 realyorkshire.co.uk

6 For heaths and modern art

Zennor to St Ives, Cornwall (11 miles/6 hours*)

Base your weekend in the intriguing hamlet of Zennor at The Tinners Arms, a cosy pub with four light, stylish B&B rooms next door at The

White House. This walk takes you on a savagely beautiful section of the Cornish coast and allows you to nose around arty St Ives en route, then walk back through fields to the pub. Take water and snacks to keep you going – this is a long walk. (*Plus time at St Ives.)

ROUTE From The Tinners Arms in Zennor, take the South West Coast Path to St Ives, which lands you on Porthmeor Beach, home to Tate St Ives. To return, leave town by Higher Stennack and take the field path to Zennor via Venton Vision Farm, Trevalgan and Boscubben. Look out for the kooky Wayside Museum and the carved bench-end mermaid in the churct at Zennor plus seals and stunning views along the cliffs.

MAP OS Explorer 102, Land's End

INFO St Ives Tourist Information 01736 796297 stives.co.uk, or visitcornwall.com

STAY The Tinners Arms 01736 796927 tinnersarms.com

Right: Carbis Bay, Cornwall

Old Custom House, King's Lynn, Norfolk

INFO 0845 2255121
visitscotland.com
STAY Rooms@25, 01333
313306, roomsat25.co.uk,
or any of the coastal villages
on the path, 01334 474609
(St Andrews Tourist
Information)
visitscotland.com

7 For whales and ruins
Crail to Shell Bay, Fife
(9 miles/5 hours)
This stretch of the 93-mile
Fife Coastal Path makes
comfortable walking, with
the fishing villages of Elie,
Anstruther, St Monans and
Crail offering diverting
stopping-off points.
Rooms@25 in Pittenweem
is a great little B&B, where
the rooms are smart and
comfortable and the
welcome warm. In between
are stretches of rocky and
sandy coastline peppered
with architectural ruins
and geological features,
including the extraordinary
sandstone Caiplie Caves.
Seals, dolphins and whales
have all been spotted so
keep your binoculars to
hand. Stop off at the award-
winning Anstruther Fish Bar
for lunch (factor in queuing
time, it's popular).
ROUTE Join the coastal path
just after Crail, passing The
Pans and the Caiplie Caves,
until you reach Anstruther,
where the path skirts the
town and continues along
a clifftop to Pittenweem.
Walk through St Monans.
Continue past ruined
Ardross Castle, through Elie,
past its lighthouse and on to
the beach. Walk to Earlsferry
beach, where you can take
the Chain Walk (a bit hairy!
– steps carved into the cliff
and chains to cling to) or the
clifftop path. End in Shell
Bay, near the caravan park.
MAP OS Explorer 371,
St Andrews & East Fife.
Landranger 59, St Andrews

8 For seabirds and solitude
King's Lynn, Norfolk to
Sutton Bridge, Lincs (13
miles/6 hours)
Seabirds, huge skies and
solitude are the highlights of
this walk, which is on the
margins of the great Wash
Estuary. There's also a chance
to explore the salty old port
of King's Lynn during your
weekend stay in the stylish,
welcoming and upmarket
Bank House Hotel, set on
the historic quayside, which
serves excellent locally
sourced food.
ROUTE Take the ferry to West
Lynn, then follow the Peter
Scott Walk round the sea
wall to the lighthouse (where
Scott lived in the 1930s).
From here, follow the east
bank of the River Nene and
cross to Sutton Bridge. Catch
the Norfolk Green bus 505
back to King's Lynn. Look out

for the view of King's Lynn from the West Lynn ferry, plus the vast skies and wild birds that swoop over the Wash.
MAP OS Explorer 249, Spalding & Holbeach
INFO King's Lynn Tourist Information 01553 763044 visitwestnorfolk.com or visiteastofengland.com
STAY Bank House Hotel 01553 660492 thebankhouse.co.uk, or elsewhere in King's Lynn 01553 763044 visitwestnorfolk.com

9 For vampires and venerable inns

Whitby to High Hawsker, N Yorks (8 miles/4 hours) Follow the Dracula Trail through Whitby, then walk out along cliffs where jet was once mined. Enjoy Whitby's Captain Cook Memorial Museum on the harbour and spoil yourself with some jet jewellery from the town's workshops. The venerable White Horse & Griffin inn is wonderfully welcoming, with a laid-back style that enchants its many fans. The friendly and witty staff will happily point you towards the delights of Whitby.
ROUTE Starting at the White Horse & Griffin, simply stroll out of the inn door. From Whitby Abbey, follow the Cleveland Way national trail along the cliffs for three miles to Gnipe Howe, passing Saltwick Bay en route. Go inland to High Hawsker, then take the old railway footpath back

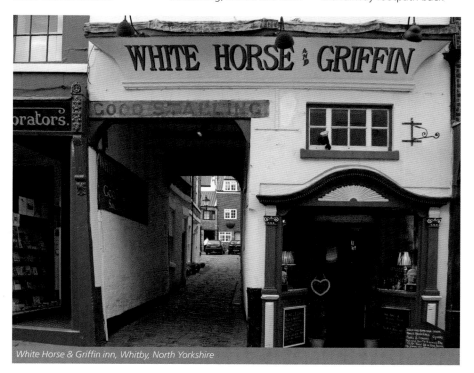

White Horse & Griffin inn, Whitby, North Yorkshire

to Whitby. Look out for settings from *Dracula* – the 199 steps, St Mary's Church and Whitby Abbey, the view from the cliffs and Larpool Viaduct.

MAP OS Landranger 27, North York Moors

INFO Whitby Tourist Information 01723 383636 discoveryorkshirecoast.com. Captain Cook Memorial Museum 01947 601900 cookmuseumwhitby.co.uk

STAY White Horse & Griffin 01947 604857 whitehorseandgriffin.co.uk

10 For cliffs and grandeur
Birling Gap to Beachy Head, East Sussex (5 miles/2 hours)

Embark upon an exhilarating, vertiginous walk at the brink of Britain's tallest chalk cliffs. Then rest your limbs at a classic seafront hotel, the Grand, a beautifully restored example of Victorian 'wedding cake' architecture. Every comfort is to hand at the hotel – swimming pool, sauna, steam room,

massages and manicures; it's family friendly, too. Look out for seasonal spa breaks and seasonal packages.

ROUTE From the hotel, take an open-topped bus or the number 13 service to Beachy Head car park (by road, it's signed off the A259 from Newhaven to Eastbourne). From here, take the cliff path to Birling Gap, then return inland by Hodcombe Farm and West Brow to catch the bus home. Look out for the view from Beachy Head, which is 530 feet tall, and

Three Cliffs Bay, Gower

marvel at Belle Toute lighthouse, which was moved 50 feet inland in 1999 to save it from toppling over the cliffs.

MAP OS Explorer 123, Eastbourne & Beachy Head
INFO Eastbourne Tourist Information 0871 663 0031 visiteastbourne.com
STAY Grand Hotel 01323 412345 grandeastbourne.com

11 For rocky strands and sheer indulgence

West Cliff to Three Cliffs Bay, Gower
(7 miles/4 hours)

Take a walk among Gower's wonderful beaches, caves, rock arches, cliffs and sands – ending up at Three Cliffs Bay, if you can tear yourself away from the luxurious embrace of Fairyhill Hotel, near Reynoldston (15 minutes' drive away). An 18th century house, set in 24 acres of parkland, it has eight individually designed bedrooms and an award-winning restaurant, featuring Gower-raised lamb and locally caught fish.

ROUTE NB This is a low tide walk. Check gowerlive.co.uk for the tide times. From West Cliff car park, walk to Pobbles beach and turn right, passing Three Cliffs Bay. Cross the stepping stones over Pennard Pill (OS ref 538883), then make a circuit of Penmaen Burrows. Head to North Hills Farm. Cross and recross the A4118. Pass Pennard Castle and Pennard Burrows to West Cliff. Look out for the rock arch on Pobbles beach and the ruins of Pennard Castle.

MAP OS Explorer 164, Gower
INFO Mumbles Tourist Information 01792 361302 mumblestic.co.uk
STAY Fairyhill Hotel 01792 390139 fairyhill.net

12 For wild moors and whisky

Knockinaam Lodge to Portpatrick, Galloway
(8½ miles, 4½ hours)

Few walkers bother with the hammerhead peninsula of the Rhins of Galloway, and more fool them – here in the south-westernmost corner of Scotland are beautiful cliffs, wild moors and a peach of a cosy hotel. Knockinaam Lodge, snug in its secluded slip of a bay, is the perfect getaway spot.

This is the heart of sporting and walking country so they don't just tolerate guests returning muddy, wet and ravenous – they expect it. Chef Tony Pierce uses locally caught fish to great effect, and after a long walk, you'll appreciate his sinful puddings. Cheerful fires and more than 120 malt whiskies await your attention.

ROUTE From Knockinaam Lodge, follow the coast to Dunskey Castle and on to Portpatrick. Next, take the Southern Upland Way to Port Mora and Port Kale, and return to Portpatrick. Head inland to Merrick Hill and from there, make your way back to Knockinaam through Portree Bridge and Port o' Spittal. Look out for haunted Dunskey Castle, maritime memorials in Old Kirk, Portpatrick and pioneer telephone cable pavilions at Port Kale.

MAP OS Explorer 309, Stranraer & The Rhins
INFO Stranraer Tourist Information 01776 702595 visitscotland.com
STAY Knockinaam Lodge 01776 810471 knockinaamlodge.com

Weekends for dog lovers

There is nothing more exciting for a dog than to run along an endless sandy beach and have the opportunity to splash in and out of gentle waves. It's a joy for dog owners too, but dogs are sometimes banned on some of our best beaches. Do not fear, we have identified lots of coastal places where dogs and their owners are welcome. Remember to do your bit by following local signage, keeping the lead on when asked and sticking to the 'bag and bin' rule, to ensure you'll always be welcome back.

This page: Room to run, Isle of Tiree, Inner Hebrides

1 For the family pooch

Amble Links, Amble, Northumberland

Dogs and children will love pootling about the rockpools on this sand, rock and shingle beach backed by cliffs on the northern edge of Druridge Bay. The seven-mile-long beach is popular with birdspotters, too – waders and diving ducks abound in the network of freshwater ponds and habitats that have been created from re-landscaped, open-cast mines inland. A mile offshore you can see the 80-foot lighthouse on Coquet Island, which is an RSPB reserve for puffins, terns, elder ducks and roseate terns. You can't land but you can cruise round it with Puffin Cruises and well-controlled dogs with sturdy sea legs are welcome aboard too.
INFO 01665 511333 visitalnwick.org.uk or 01665 712313 ambletouristinformation. co.uk. Puffin Cruises 01665 711975
STAY In Amble or nearby Warkworth 01665 712313 visitnorthumberland.com.

Standing guard at Beer, Devon

Pet-friendly Welcome Cottages 0845 268 0817 welcomecottages.com

2 For old sea dogs

Beer, Devon

One of the most sheltered positions on the coast made this small pebble cove, surrounded by high white cliffs, a smugglers' haven. Today, it's a quieter place with plenty of opportunity to take the air and admire the view without too much strenuous walking, so it's perfect for old faithfuls who may prefer a leisurely pace. Dogs are allowed on the East Beach to the left of the slipway or you can admire the fishing boats in the harbour from the garden of the Anchor Inn in Fore

Street. If you are feeling more energetic, climb the South West Coast Path that runs through the village to Beer Head for the view to Seaton.
INFO Seaton Tourist Information 01297 21660 seatontic.com. Anchor Inn 01297 20386 anchorinn-beer.co.uk
STAY In Beer or nearby Seaton 01297 21660 seatontic.com, or devon-online.com

3 For sociable surfers

Penhale Sands, Perranporth, Cornwall
Let your mutt feel the wind in its tail on this three-mile stretch of sand, famed for its clean water and surf. Dogs 'under control' can have the run of the place, are welcome, on a lead, at bar and restaurant The Watering Hole, and will have fun sniffing out the buried ruins of an oratory built by the patron saint of Cornwall, St Piran, in the dunes. In July and August, dogs must be on leads. Dog wastebins are provided. Parking and toilets nearby.
INFO 01872 575254

perranporthinfo.co.uk. The Watering Hole 01872 572888 the-wateringhole.co.uk
STAY In Perranporth or St Agnes 01872 575254 perranporthinfo.co.uk or 01872 322900 visitcornwall.com

4 For nature lovers

Murlough, Dundrum, County Down
This long, sandy beach in the shadow of the mountains of Mourne offers a perfect dog-friendly escape and dogs are welcome to most parts of the reserve, including the main boardwalk. Two dogs can stay at the National Trust's Murlough Cottage at Dundrum and explore the 6,000-year-old sand dune

system that, together with woodland and heathland, forms the Murlough National Nature Reserve. Spot common and grey seals in summer and autumn and watch some of the thousands of wildfowl and waders that stop off here in winter. When ground-nesting birds are breeding or cattle are grazing, there are a few doggie restrictions so check the signs locally.
INFO Murlough National Nature Reserve 028 4375 1467 nationaltrust.org/murlough
STAY In Dundrum or nearby Newcastle 028 4372 2222 discovernorthernireland.com or downdc.gov.uk. National Trust Cottages 0844 8002078 nationaltrustcottages.co.uk

Murlough Nature Reserve, County Down

5 For a dog-friendly pub

Winterton-on-Sea, Norfolk
Frustration at not being able to find a pub where her family and their dog Millie could eat together drove Kate Crosby to set up her 'guide to happy eating out with your dog' (doggiepubs. co.uk). The site awards three doggie stars to the 300-year-old Fisherman's Return in this picturesque Norfolk village close to long stretches of sandy beach and beautiful walks across the Winterton Dunes National Nature Reserve, where you can spot terns, natterjack toads and seals. Well-behaved dogs are welcome everywhere in the pub, including the B&B rooms, and a water bowl and treats are always available for them.
INFO The Fisherman's Return 01493 393305 fishermans-return.com. Natural England Enquiry Service 0845 600 3078 naturalengland.org.uk
STAY In Winterton-on-Sea or nearby Caister-on-Sea 01493 846346 great-yarmouth.co.uk

Left: Tilly hitches a ride at Durdle Door, Dorset

Out for a run at Camber Sands, East Sussex

6 For little dogs

Camber Sands, East Sussex
The late, lamented writer, film-maker and environmentalist Roger Deakin describes visiting this sand-blown beach in his book *Waterlog*, the tale of his swim around Britain: 'I seemed to be the only person lacking a dog, and the only man without a bunch of keys dangling from my belt. What with the dogs and keys, it looked and sounded like a Securicor outing. [Locals] appeared to favour little dogs: Cairn terriers, poodles, dachshunds, the occasional Jack Russell.' Yet Deakin escapes for a solitary 'two-and-a-half-hour barefoot hike along the shoreline'. From May to September, dogs are restricted on some parts of the beach and must be on leads elsewhere. Dog bins are provided.
INFO Rye Tourist Information 01797 229049 visitrye.co.uk
STAY In Camber or nearby Rye 01797 229049 visitrye.co.uk

7 For a long run

Village Beach, Woolacombe, Devon
There's plenty of space for even the leggiest hound on three miles of golden sand sandwiched between two dramatic peninsulas – Baggy and Morte Points – and backed by hills and the Woolacombe Downs. From April to November, there is a section of beach that dogs are not allowed on (check maps at the beach entrance),

but everywhere else they can be exercised freely.
INFO 01271 870553 woolacombetourism.co.uk
STAY In Woolacombe or nearby Ilfracombe 01271 870553 woolacombetourism.co.uk, or visitdevon.co.uk

8 For solitary stomps
Balmedie, Aberdeen, Aberdeenshire
Sand, sea and skylarks – there are some five miles of sandy beach and grassy dunes at Balmedie and seldom a soul in sight. But if you are more sociably inclined, dogs are welcome on some guided walks led by Balmedie Country Park rangers (for details, call 01358 726417). Work up an appetite looking for shells and spotting wild flowers, then have a picnic. From April to September you can hire one of the barbecues provided; bring your own charcoal. Call 01467 628261 to book.

INFO Aberdeen Tourist Information 01224 288828 agtb.org
STAY In Balmedie, Potterton or Newburgh 01224 288828 (Aberdeen Tourist Information) agtb.org

9 For cliff walks
Abereiddy Bay, Abereiddy, Pembrokeshire
Canine appreciation of the sunsets enjoyed from this west-facing beach may be limited, but any dog worth his seasalt will love the cliff

Abereiddy Bay, Pembrokeshire

walks from Abereiddy to Porthgain, one of the best stretches of the Pembrokeshire Coast Path. The dark sand on the slipway beach is made from pounded grey slate, and minerals exposed during quarrying colour the waters of the 'Blue Lagoon' just to the north. Parking and toilets available. Garn Isaf offers dog-friendly B&B and a self-catering cottage and camping nearby.

INFO Oriel y Parc Information Centre 01437 720392 orielyparc.co.uk, or St David's Tourist Information 01437 720392 stdavidsinfo.org.uk
STAY In Abereiddy or St David's visitpembrokeshire.com. Garn Isaf B&B 01348 831838 garnisaf.com

10 For mongrels
Durdle Door, West Lulworth, Dorset
Timothy, Enid Blyton's 'big brown mongrel dog with an absurdly long tail' of fictional Famous Five fame, had many adventures bounding about on Dorset beaches, such as this narrow strand of mixed shingle, gravel and sand leading to the sea-eroded limestone arch of Durdle Door. Dogs of all shapes and sizes will enjoy the circular walks from the South West Coastal Path (walking guides from Lulworth Cove Heritage Centre). And when you've walked enough, you and your dog are welcome at The Castle Inn in West Lulworth – it even has a dedicated doggie page on its website. There are comfortable, dog-friendly B&B rooms too.

INFO Lulworth Estate 01929 400352 lulworth.com
STAY The Castle Inn 01929 400 311 thecastleinn-lulworthcove.co.uk, or elsewhere in Lulworth or nearby Swanage 01929 552740 visitswanageandpurbeck.co.uk

11 For varied scenery
Benllech, Anglesey
Clean bathing waters, watersports and proximity to the Anglesey Coastal Path make this Blue flag beach a favourite with dog-owning families. Some areas are off limits from May to September but there's still plenty of space to run around after a ball, and food is available at cafés and restaurants right beside the beach. The path takes in sea cliffs, sandy and rocky shores, so there's lots for you and your pooch to explore.

INFO Llanfair PG Tourist Information 01248 713177 visitanglesey.co.uk
STAY In Benllech, Red Wharf Bay or Pentraeth 01248 713177 visitanglesey.co.uk, or visitwales.co.uk

12 For dune exploring
Holywell Bay, Cornwall
Not far from Newquay is Holywell Bay, where you and your four-legged friend can explore many of the natural delights including rolling dunes – rising in some places to a height of up to 60 metres – plus myriad rockpools and a stream that runs through the beach to the sea. The location of the 'holy well' that gave the beach its name is of much debate – some say it is a grotto-like cave carved out by the sea. At low tide, just off the beach, a 70-year-old shipwreck emerges from the sea. The beach is easy to

Playing catch-up on the sand, Cornwall

get to and dogs can be walked here all year, providing they are kept under control. You can download a recommended six-mile wildlife walk (entitled Cubert, Cornwall) that takes in the dunes, from the National Trust website.
INFO National Trust Cornwall 01208 265200 nationaltrust.org.uk
STAY In Holywell or Newquay 01637 854020 visitnewquay.org or visitcornwall.co.uk

13 For a stroll at sunset

Old Hunstanton, Norfolk

Old Hunstanton may be an east coast village but, unusually, it's one that faces west so it enjoys some fine sunsets. The cliffs, some 18 metres high, have fascinating stripes of chalk and stone running through them and the sandy beach is a good place to look for fossils. A long strip of sand, popular with kite surfers, is often relatively quiet, so it's

perfect for a good long leg-stretch with your canine friend. There are no dog restrictions on the beach. The village is interesting too, with seaside cottages, an art/crafts gallery and a church dating back to the early 13th century.
INFO 01485 532610 visitwestnorfolk.com, or tournorfolk.co.uk
STAY In Old Hunstanton or Hunstanton 01485 532610 visitwestnorfolk.com

Right: A quick dip in Pembrokeshire

Crabs

Rocky seashores are perfect for spying on these little nippers. Just go to the margin between the high and low tide and use this guide to help you identify the most common types. Lift

Chinese Mitten Crab

Eriocheir sinensis

DISTINGUISHING MARKS

A spindly, olive-brown crab with oddly shaped claws that are used for lifting stones.

WHERE TO SPOT More common in brackish estuaries, such as the Thames and Humber, than on the coast.

A CURIOUS THING This is an alien invader, which can cause damage to riverbanks.

Edible Crab

Cancer pagurus

DISTINGUISHING MARKS

A bulky, orange/brown crab with a pie-crust edge to its shell (or carapace) and chunky black claws.

WHERE TO SPOT In pools and beneath crevices on shores around the UK. Look low down on the shore near the sea.

A CURIOUS THING Living up to 20 years, it can crush all kinds of shellfish with its powerful claws.

Velvet Swimming Crab

Necora puber

DISTINGUISHING MARKS

Purple-blue in colour, with long claws and distinctive bright red eyes. Its paddle-like back legs help it to swim well.

WHERE TO SPOT Low down on rocky shorelines all around the UK.

A CURIOUS THING Possibly the most ferocious species, it is often nicknamed the 'devil crab'.

and replace any rocks carefully as you go – crabs and other rockpool dwellers need the rocks for protection. Crabs have to shed their hard shells periodically as they grow – look out for these discarded shells at the shoreline. And why do they walk sideways? It's because of the way their legs bend, being specially adapted for squeezing into crevices to evade their predators.

Hermit Crab
Pagurus bernhardus

DISTINGUISHING MARKS The shell (which originates from a snail) is its most recognisable feature. If you are patient, you might see a set of small legs and stalked eyes peering out of it.

WHERE TO SPOT All around the UK in rockpools and in deeper water.

A CURIOUS THING If you place a suitable empty shell nearby, it will swap 'home' before your very eyes.

Spiny Spider Crab
Maja squinado

DISTINGUISHING MARKS Its spiny shell – often totally covered in seaweed – and long, spindly legs make this an intriguing-looking creature.

WHERE TO SPOT Most common on the south and west coasts.

A CURIOUS THING They can gather in their thousands in shallow bays during spring and summer.

Common Shore Crab
Carcinus maenas

DISTINGUISHING MARKS This is the crab you're most likely to see. It comes in a range of patterns and colours, but is most often a mottled green.

WHERE TO SPOT In any shallow waters, including estuaries, around the UK.

A CURIOUS THING You might find seemingly 'dead' crabs, but these are often just 'skins' discarded in the summer moult.

Weekends for wildlife

Our coastline offers some of the richest bird- and wildlife-watching possibilities in Britain and, if you know where to look, you can be seal-spotting one minute and photographing puffins the next. As the tide goes down, many seabirds flock to the shore to forage for food; and estuaries play host to waders, while high cliffs offer safe nesting sites for breeding colonies. Offshore, you can revel in the antics of porpoises and dolphins. Grab your binoculars and our recommendations and head for these tried and tested hotspots.

This page: I spy, with a telescope

1 For seabirds

St Cuthbert's Cove, Farne Islands, Northumberland

In the April to early August breeding season, 100,000 seabirds congregate on the cliffs, stacks and grassy tops of these rocky outposts, two and a half miles off the north coast of Northumberland.
The numbers of puffins, guillemots, shags and the UK's fastest flying duck, the eider, are swelled by spring and autumn migrants, such as the rare roseate tern. Human visitors can boat over from Seahouses to land on Inner Farne, Staple Island and Longstone, but the islands' owner, the National Trust, advises wearing a hat to prevent being pecked on the head by dive-bombing Arctic terns protecting their young.
INFO National Trust 01665 720651 nationaltrust.org.uk
STAY In Seahouses or nearby Bamburgh 01655 720884 visitnorthumberland.com

2 For rare choughs

Porth Neigwl (Hell's Mouth), Pwllheli, Gwynedd

Recognisable by its red bill and legs, and a distinctive 'kee-aw' call, the chough is the symbol of the Llyn Peninsula Area of Outstanding Natural Beauty. The presence of the crow-like bird is also one of the reasons for the area's status as a SSSI (Site of Special Scientific Interest). There are fewer than 500 pairs of choughs breeding in the UK, and 60 are to be found on Llyn. Feeding on the insect life from the gorse, heather and hedgerows around this popular surfing beach at the tip of the peninsula, the chough entertains with diving and swooping aerial displays.
INFO Pwllheli Tourist Information 01758 613000, or llyn.info
STAY In Pwllheli or nearby Abersoch 01758 613000 pwllheli.org.uk, or visitsnowdonia.info

3 For dolphin-spotting

New Quay, Cardigan Bay, Cardigan

One of two UK sites (the other is the Moray Firth) to support populations of bottlenose dolphins, there are regular sightings in Cardigan Bay. Look out for them on a calm day between April and the end of October, from either the pier at New Quay or along

Bottlenose dolphins, Cardigan Bay

Guillemots and gulls, Farne Islands, Northumberland

asparagus fields, are now a haven for the native red squirrel (Squirrel Nutkin is known to be partial to pine seeds). Unfortunately the Formby reds suffered from an outbreak of squirrel pox, a virus borne by its American grey cousins, which swept through the area in 2007/08. However, a successful breeding season in 2009 saw numbers rise back to over 200 in the Sefton Coast Woodlands area and conservationists are optimistic that the autumn counts this year will show further increases. Catching a glimpse of a red bushy tail will set you on your way along the Sefton Coastal Path with a spring in your step.

INFO National Trust Formby 01704 878591 nationaltrust.org.uk

STAY In Formby or nearby Southport 01704 533333 visitsouthport.com or visitliverpool.com

Rock Street, the closest of the New Quay terraces to the sea. If you do want to go out on a boat, join a Dolphin Survey Boat Trip to help support the research work of the Cardigan Bay Marine Wildlife Centre. Book at the centre in New Quay.

INFO Cardigan Bay Marine Wildlife 01545 560032 cbmwc.org

STAY In New Quay or nearby Aberaeron 01545 560865 tourism.ceredigion.gov.uk

4 For red squirrels
Freshfield, Formby, Merseyside

Pinewoods, planted at Formby Point 100 years ago to protect Formby's

5 For eagles
Laggan Sands, Lochbuie, Isle of Mull

Dubbed 'Eagle Island' by birdwatchers, Mull is one of the best places in the UK to spot golden eagles and white-tailed sea eagles. The largest raptor in northern Europe (and the fourth largest in the world), the white-tailed sea eagle has a pale head, a short, white, wedge-shaped tail and an immense pair of broad wings measuring up to 2.45 metres. More of a coast hunting species than the golden eagle, it skims the surface of the freshwater loch to catch fish with its sharp talons. Golden eagles have a characteristic golden head, a longer, rectangular tail and narrower wings, held in a shallow V-shape in flight.

INFO Craignure Visitor Information 01680 812377 holidaymull.co.uk
STAY Laggan Farm B&B 01680 814206 lagganfarm.co.uk, or elsewhere in Craignure 01680 812377 or 08707 200 610 visitscotland.com

6 For harbour porpoises
Strangford Lough, County Down
One of the smallest marine mammals, the harbour or common porpoise is often confused with a dolphin, but is smaller (around two metres long), shyer and rarely surfaces except to breathe. But in the sheltered tidal waters of the UK's largest sea inlet, you may well spot the distinctive rounded, snub-nosed heads of *Phocoena phocoena*. The Look Out, on the eastern shore of the lough, just north of the village of Greyabbey, in the grounds of the National Trust's Mount Stewart House and Gardens, provides information. Or, to paddle with the porpoises, check out the Strangford Lough Canoe Trail.
INFO 028 4278 7823 strangfordlough.org and nationaltrust.org.uk. Canoe Trail 028 9030 3930 canoeni.com
STAY In Strangford or nearby Portaferry 028 9182 6846 discovernorthernireland.com

7 For sea lavender
Saltfleetby to Theddlethorpe Dunes, Lincolnshire
In late summer, the saltmarsh on the northern end of this five-mile coastal reserve stretching between Mablethorpe North End and Saltfleet Haven is a purple haze of sea lavender. One of the prettiest and tallest coastal flowering plants, sea lavender flowers from July to late October. Also known as marsh rosemary, the flower can be grown and dried for use in winter bouquets and to keep away moths. Natural England organises guided walks on the reserve: the Paradise Trail takes in the saltmarshes.
INFO Natural England 0845 600 3078 naturalengland.org.uk
STAY In Mablethorpe or Sutton on Sea 01507 474939 visitlincolnshire.com

8 For big fish
Niarbyl Bay, Dalby, Isle of Man
The southern and south-western coast of the Isle of Man is a basking shark hotspot: on a calm sunny day train your binoculars and you may be rewarded with the mirror-like flash of a wet dorsal fin. Many sightings have been recorded within 1km of this rocky outcrop between mid-May and mid-August. From

Right: Wild flowers such as sea thrift thrive at the coast

Atlantic puffins taking a breather in the Farne Islands

10 For starling formations

Marazion Marsh, near Penzance, Cornwall

The largest reed bed in Cornwall is within view of St Michael's Mount, just off the coast. Migrating warblers start arriving in spring, when the reeds and flowers are at their most abundant. A spectacular winter sight – although it doesn't happen every year, so call ahead to find out – is the mass flocking of starlings. Peregrines, buzzards and sparrowhawks join in, on the lookout for easy meals. You'll see other birds, too, including herons, chiffchaffs, water rails and little egrets. Bitterns are now regular winter visitors as well.
INFO Marazion Marsh Reserve 01736 711682 rspb.org.uk
STAY In Marazion or nearby Penzance 01736 362207 visitcornwall.com

the clifftop, if the water is clear, you may even see the shark's white mouth as it feeds just under the surface of the water. But be warned: a seal's head bobbing upright can also give you a *Jaws* moment...
INFO 01624 686766 visitisleofman.com. Manx Wildlife Trust 01624 801985 manxbaskingsharkwatch.com
STAY In Port St Mary or nearby Peel 01624 686766 visitisleofman.com

9 For seal-spotting

Blakeney Point, Blakeney, Norfolk

Seeing seals is never guaranteed but the boats that take tourists out on this sand and shingle spit, part of the National Trust's Blakeney National Nature Reserve, will give you a very good chance of striking lucky. Some 500 common and grey seals haul out onto the sandbanks at the far end of the Point. Numbers peak in August when they are moulting and you may even see a few common seal pups. Some boat trips land on the Point: visit the Old Lifeboat House, now a National Trust Information Centre.
INFO National Trust Information Centre 01263 740241 nationaltrust.org.uk
STAY In Blakeney or nearby Wells-Next-the-Sea 01328 710885 (March–October) and 01263 512497 visitnorthnorfolk.com

11 For wild otters

Haroldswick, Unst, Shetland

Naturalist Simon King raised the profile of Shetland's wildlife with his recent BBC2 TV programme and book

(*Shetland Diaries*), but the exact locations of where the island's elusive wild otters live, play, swim and hunt remain a closely guarded secret. Wildlife guide John Campbell of Shetland Otters took King to film otters in a tidal lagoon on Shetland's north-east mainland at 5am. Shetland is one of the few places in the UK that wild otters can regularly be seen during daylight hours. Low tide at Haroldswick on Unst, the most northerly inhabited island of the UK (population 614), is as good a place as any to spot this protected species but all of Shetland's sheltered sea inlets are good otter-watching locations.
INFO Shetland Otters 01806 577358 shetlandotters.com. Unst Tourist Information unst.org or undiscoveredscotland.co.uk/unst
STAY In Haroldswick 01595 989898 visit.shetland.org, or 0845 22 55 121 visitscotland.com

12 For summer migrants
Dungeness Nature Reserve, Kent
Dotted with trails, hides and swathes of shingle, this reserve offers a clear view of migratory birds arriving and leaving these shores. Masses of swallows pass by en route to warmer climes in August and September; and there are colonies of seabirds, breeding ducks and wintering wildfowl. Look out for shovellers, pintails and gadwalls and, in winter, smew, which are particularly smart little black and white ducks. There are breeding bitterns and marsh harriers here, too. Open daily except 25 and 26 December.
INFO Dungeness Nature Reserve 01797 320588 rspb.org.uk
STAY At the Dungeness Bird

Mass flocking of starlings at Marazion Marsh, Cornwall

Observatory 01797 321309 dungenessbirdobs.org.uk, or in nearby Camber Sands or Rye 01797 229049 visitrye.co.uk

13 For puffins and gannets

Bempton Cliffs, near Bridlington, East Yorkshire
From March right through to October, these dramatic chalky cliffs are home to 200,000 breeding seabirds, including everyone's favourite, the puffin. Five clifftop observation points allow great views of them, all busy incubating eggs, nestling chicks or hunting food (watch for puffins with eels dangling from their beaks as they return to the nest). The puffins leave in July but autumn brings migrants and the clifftop habitats can be alive with warblers, chats and flycatchers. Bempton is also home to the UK's largest mainland gannetry. Summer is the best time to watch these birds, which are large and white with black wing tips and have a wingspan of six feet! In strong winds they look stunning as they hang

almost motionless in the air. INFO Bempton Cliffs Visitor Centre 01262 851179 rspb.org.uk STAY In Bridlington 01262 673474 bridlington.co.uk or nearby Filey 01723 383636, discoveryorkshirecoast.com

14 For terns and peregrine falcons

St Catherine's Point, Isle of Wight
The Isle of Wight is a pleasure for birdwatchers, with firecrests and nightjars among the frequent spots in the Island's forests. With more than 50 miles of heritage coast, the usual suspects of seabirds breed here (cormorants, kittiwakes, razorbills), and you might see a common or sandwich tern. The best place for birdspotting is from the hides at Newtown Creek and if you head for St Catherine's Point, you might be fortunate enough to see the resident peregrine falcons in action, speeding with unbelievable agility through the air. INFO IoW Tourist Information 01983 813813 islandbreaks.co.uk STAY In Ventnor or nearby

Bonchurch 01983 813813 islandbreaks.co.uk

15 For wading birds

Snettisham Bird Reserve, Norfolk
The hides at this RSPB reserve are perfectly placed to take advantage of high tides. On high spring tides, thousands of wading birds retreat towards the hides, giving you pole-position views of knot, redshank and oystercatchers to name a few. Dawn and dusk bring treats, too – barn owls hunt over the reserve, and in summer, keep an eye out for avocet chicks with their long legs and upturned beaks, out to feed with their graceful parents. At dawn or dusk from late autumn to midwinter the skies can be filled with pink-footed geese. INFO Snettisham Bird Reserve 01485 54268 rspb.org.uk STAY In Snettisham or nearby Hunstanton 01485 532610 (Hunstanton Tourist Information) visitwestnorfolk.com

Right: Boat trips take visitors out to see common seals at Blakeney Point, Norfolk

Weekends for seaside pubs

Why is it that a harbour view or a beachside garden seems to make all the difference to the taste of a pub drink? Could it be the thirst you work up as you tramp along the shore to get there? Or maybe it's the invigorating quality of the sea air when you arrive? Whatever it is, there's no doubt that British seaside pubs score very highly indeed on our popularity list. Many of them serve very good food too, and offer excellent overnight accommodation, so there's no need to stray far from beach to bar to bed.

This page: Spyglass Inn, Ventnor, Isle of Wight

1 For photography enthusiasts

The Old Inn, Wester Ross

Take the camera if you visit the west Highland town of Gairloch in winter. Sandy beaches and views towards Skye and the Western Isles inspire, while, further inland, chances are you'll spot red deer. After a day out, gather at The Old Inn, with its terrace overlooking the water. It offers a wonderful selection of single malt whiskies and local real ales, including An Teallach. They now have their own custom-built microbrewery too. Fresh local seafood, game and fish dishes figure highly on the menu. You can stay over in one of the comfortable rooms, some of which have a sea view. INFO The Old Inn 0800 542 5444 theoldinn.net
STAY In Gairloch or nearby villages in Wester Ross 0845 2255121 visitscotland.com

2 For beach cricket

The Ship Inn, Elie, Fife

If you fancy a game of beach cricket, pack your pads and gloves, for they take it seriously at The Ship Inn in Elie, on the northern side of

Beach cricket at The Ship Inn, Elie, Fife

the Firth of Forth. At low tide in the summer months, the Blue Flag beach opposite this 19th century inn doubles up as a cricket pitch for the inn's first XI, playing challengers from other parts of Scotland and beyond. Any batsman who hits a six into the inn's garden gets a bottle of wine. The Ship is also noted for its food, with summer barbecues a speciality on the terrace overlooking the beach, so once you tire of watching grown men throwing a ball at each other, it might be time for something char-grilled or perhaps a seafood platter. INFO The Ship Inn 01333 330246 ship-elie.com

3 For après surf

**The Driftwood Spars,
St Agnes, Cornwall**
This pub/hotel was originally
built in the 17th century and
during its long life has been
a chandlers, a warehouse
and a billet for war evacuees.
Down the road is
Trevaunance Cove, which
is popular with surfers.
After catching a few
righteous waves, return to
the Spars for its own brewed
beer and locally sourced
food, including gourmet
burgers. The pub has a
reputation for live music –
Queen played here before
becoming superstars.
INFO Trevaunance Cove,
St Agnes, Cornwall
01872 552428,
driftwoodspars.com
STAY In St Agnes or
nearby Perranporth
01872 322900
visitcornwall.com

4 For harbour views

**The Rising Sun, Lynmouth,
Devon**
This medieval thatched pub
and hotel overlooks the
harbour and Lynmouth
Bay and the spectacular
hogsback cliffs. The inn has
been on this spot since the
14th century and gradually
the adjoining cottages have
been taken over to create
the hotel. In times past,
contrabrand arrived here
from the West Indies and
America, and legend has
it there is a secret tunnel
somewhere. The cottages
used to be fishermen's
homes and they have
interesting crooked
staircases, narrow
passageways and
creaking floors. Most of
the rooms have a sea view.
INFO The Rising Sun
01598 753223
risingsunlynmouth.co.uk
STAY In Lynmouth or nearby
Porlock 01598 752225
lyntourism.co.uk

5 For armchair sailors

**The Ship Inn, Red Wharf
Bay, Anglesey**
If you enjoy watching sailors
mucking around with
mainbraces, the beer garden
at The Ship is the perfect
spot on a warm day. Several
hundred years old and run
by the same family since
1971, this quayside inn
offers marvellous views of
the north-west coast of
Anglesey. Small craft and
yachts are drawn by the
good food, such as the
chef's celebrated fish pie.

The Ship Inn, Red Wharf Bay, Anglesey

In winter, there are cosy log fires.

INFO The Ship Inn
01248 852568
shipinnredwharfbay.co.uk
STAY In Red Wharf Bay or nearby Benllech 01248 713177 visitanglesey.co.uk

6 For a view of the Channel

The Coastguard, St Margaret's Bay, Dover, Kent

With the White Cliffs of Dover at its back, The Coastguard in St Margaret's Bay clings by its fingertips to England. In fact, mobile phones retune to French networks when you arrive. On a sunny day, view the ferries and tankers crossing the Channel from the terrace. Or, when a storm is raging, retreat to the bar and you'll almost believe you're out at sea. Real ales and locally sourced dishes add to the winning formula.

INFO The Coastguard 01304 853176 thecoastguard.co.uk
STAY In nearby Walmer or Deal 01304 205108, whitecliffscountry.org.uk

7 For big skies

The White Horse, Brancaster Staithe, Norfolk

Glorious big skies and the windswept saltmarshes draw artists, birdwatchers and walkers to this area. The White Horse offers a modern haven with 15 spacious rooms, while the pub serves Brancaster Brewery real ale along with other East Anglian favourites and excellent food (including local mussels and home-made bouillabaisse). Sit on the terrace and contemplate the remains of the day, knowing you haven't got far to go to bed.

INFO The White Horse
01485 210262
whitehorsebrancaster.co.uk
STAY At The White Horse, or in nearby Holkham or Wells-Next-the-Sea 01328 710885 visitnorthnorfolk.com

8 For Arthur Ransome fans

The Butt & Oyster, Pin Mill, Suffolk

In the one-time smugglers' haven of Pin Mill, where the River Orwell wends its way

The Butt & Oyster, Pin Mill, Suffolk

to the sea, The Butt & Oyster is the ideal place for watching the action on the water. A long-time meeting point for fishermen, bargemen and even Arthur Ransome (who featured it in his novel *We Didn't Mean to Go to Sea*), it is now owned by Adnams Brewery so good ales are guaranteed as are freshly caught fish dishes. Parking can be tricky – best to stop at the municipal car park at the top of Pin Mill and walk down.

INFO The Butt & Oyster 01473 780764 debeninns.co.uk/buttandoyster

STAY In nearby villages or in Ipswich 01473 258070 visitsuffolk.com or discoversuffolk.com

9 For smuggling buffs

The Ship Inn, Saltburn-by-the-Sea, North Yorkshire
Right on the beach by the crashing North Sea, The Ship Inn is just a few steps from the Cleveland Way National Trail. A classic seafarers' pub, it dates back to the 1450s, with original beams, floors and a coal fire. In the 1780s, landlord John 'King of the

The Anchor, Walberswick, Suffolk

Smugglers' Andrew reputedly hid contraband in the stables. The pub museum describes smuggling on the Yorkshire coast where gin, brandy and tea were brought from Holland and France in treacherous conditions. Now, home-made pies including fish and steak and ale, plus a warm welcome are the draw.

INFO The Ship Inn 01287 622361

STAY In Saltburn-by-the-Sea or nearby Redcar 01287 622422 visitteesvalley.co.uk

10 For coastal walks

The Fountain Head, Branscombe, Devon
Back in 2007, the container vessel *Napoli* famously sank just off Branscombe, energising a new generation of beachcombers. This ancient village is apparently the longest in England, stretching down a stunning valley to the beach. The South West Coast Path passes close by, so a pint and bite to eat at The Fountain Head, reputedly dating back to the 14th century, is the salvation of many a weary walker. Fresh crab sandwiches or beef and

The Ship Inn, Saltburn-by-the-Sea, North Yorkshire

Branoc bitter pie really hit the spot.
INFO The Fountain Head 01297 680359 fountainheadinn.com
STAY In Branscombe or nearby Seaton or Sidmouth 01297 21660 seatontic.com or devon-online.com

11 For crabbing
The Anchor, Walberswick, Suffolk

Every summer, Walberswick hosts the British Open Crabbing Championship. And, after a couple of hours' work with a line, there's no better place to relax than at The Anchor, a family-friendly village local, separated from the North Sea by a shingle bank. Walberswick is in an Area of Outstanding Natural Beauty and The Anchor has a justly deserved reputation for its food, wine and beer, with an emphasis on seasonal and local produce, such as beer- battered cod with chips. It also has eight rooms, six in the gardens, if you can't bear to tear yourself away.
INFO The Anchor 01502 722112 anchoratwalberswick.com
STAY In Walberswick or nearby Southwold 01502 724729 visit-sunrisecoast.co.uk

12 For home-brewed beer
The Ship Inn, Low Newton-by-the-Sea, Northumberland

Beer doesn't have to travel far to be served at the bar of this popular Northumbrian pub, in a picturesque, National Trust-owned former fishing village. There is a micro-brewery on the premises, so as well as excellent food (kippers from nearby Craster), try a glass of Sandcastles at Dawn or Dolly Day Dream – the ideal pick-me-up after a walk over the sands.
INFO The Ship Inn 01665 576262 shipinnewton.co.uk. National Trust 01665

576117 nationaltrust.org.uk
STAY In Low Newton-by-the-
Sea, nearby villages or
Craster 01665 720884
visitnorthumberland.co.uk

13 For walkers

**The Smugglers Inn,
Osmington Mills, Dorset**
In a valley between
Osmington Mills and the
sea, close to the South West
Coast Path, Lulworth Cove
and Durdle Door, is this
pretty 13th-century thatched
pub with breathtaking views
across Portland Bay. In the
1790s it was home to Pierre
Latour, the French leader of
a notorious band of outlaws.
Painted on the wall outside
is Rudyard Kipling's *A
Smuggler's Song*: 'brandy
for the parson/baccy for the
clerk/laces for a lady/letters
for a spy/and watch the wall,
my darling, while the

smugglers go by'.
INFO The Smugglers Inn
01305 833125
STAY At The Smugglers Inn
or in nearby Weymouth
01305 785747
visitweymouth.co.uk

14 For bookish types

**The Ship Inn, Dymchurch,
Kent**
In the 1900s, Russell
Thorndike wrote a series of
novels here about a hero
smuggler, Dr Syn, who was
a country vicar by day and
a swashbuckling smuggler
by night. What better
location than this characterful
pub, reputedly haunted,
with hidden passageways,
a garden and a terrace
facing the sea?
INFO The Ship Inn 01303
872122 shipinn.biz
STAY In Dymchurch or nearby

New Romney or Hythe
01303 258594
discoverfolkestone.co.uk

15 For local food

**The Lifeboat Inn,
Thornham, Norfolk**
Its location on the marshes,
in the picturesque village
of Thornham, means The
Lifeboat Inn is perfectly
placed to serve local fish
– look out for Brancaster
mussels and queen scallops.
In days gone by, smugglers
used the pub as a handy
place to wait for their next
batch of illegal imports
from Holland, sinking
their booty in the nearby
river to hide it from the
customs patrol.
INFO The Lifeboat Inn 01485
512236 lifeboatinn.co.uk
STAY In Thornham or nearby
Hunstanton 01485 532610
visitwestnorfolk.com

The Lifeboat Inn, Thornham, Norfolk

Weekends for eating by the shore

There are few experiences better than sitting at a table with a great sea view while tucking into fresh seafood. A day spent walking, surfing or sightseeing will give anyone an appetite and, fortunately for us, British cuisine has come a long way. From good old fresh fish and crispy chips to succulent native oysters, locally caught crab or grilled Cornish sea bass, it is possible to have a gastronomic feast anywhere along our coastline. We have found the best places to try, complete with soundtrack of rolling ocean.

This page: Sea air works up an appetite

Sustainability

Coast supports sustainable fishing, to maintain the rich variety of marine life in UK coastal waters; so when you're choosing seafood to eat, we recommend looking out for the Marine Stewardship Council (MSC) blue 'ecolabel' denoting Certified Sustainable Seafood. See msc.org for details.

Flora Tea Rooms, Dunwich, Suffolk

1 For great fish and chips

Flora Tea Rooms, Dunwich Beach, Suffolk
Named after the shipwrecked barge whose timbers were used to construct the original tea room (rebuilt in 1987), the black-tarred wooden shack sits on the shingle beach of what was East Anglia's capital before most of it was swallowed by the sea in the 14th century. Daily specials include Dover sole and lobster straight from the fisherman on the beach, and samphire when it's in season. Other fresh fish are delivered each morning from Lowestoft fish market. Work up an appetite walking on Dunwich Heath and beach –

an Area of Outstanding Natural Beauty – then you can follow your lunch with a knickerbocker glory or banana longboat. Closed late November through to beginning of March. Check ahead for exact dates.
INFO Flora Tea Rooms 01728 648433
STAY In nearby Walberswick or Southwold
01728 453637
visit-suffolkcoast.co.uk

2 For gastronomes

L'Enclume, Cavendish Street, Cartmel, Cumbria
Simon Rogan picked an unlikely spot in which to practise his cutting edge cuisine. The residents of Cumbrian villages are more familiar with pies and picnics

than 12-course tasting menus featuring dishes such as Vintage potatoes in onion ashes. But the innovative set menus, including organic produce and items foraged from the wild, in this converted smithy have become so popular that its multi-award-winning chef has abandoned the à la carte options. To sample Rogan's talents in a more conventional setting, visit Cartmel's bistro, Rogan and Company.
INFO L'Enclume 01539 536362 lenclume.co.uk
STAY At L'Enclume, or elsewhere in Cartmel or nearby Grange-over-Sands
015395 34026
grange-over-sands.com

3 For pub grub

Applecross Inn,
Applecross, Wester Ross
The views from the beer
garden towards Raasay and
the Cuillin mountains of
Skye are ample reward for
a hair-raising journey across
the 2,053-foot Bealach na
Ba pass. But what draws
people to the lively bar of
this unassuming,
whitewashed pub is the
superb local food that Judith
Fish has been dishing up for
over 20 years. There are
always daily specials, and
squat lobster, scallops,
oysters, crab and
langoustines, fresh from
Applecross Bay, are the main
attractions for seafood fans.
The inn has B&B rooms too.
INFO Applecross Inn 01520
744262 applecross.uk.com

STAY At Applecross Inn or
nearby 0845 2255121
visitscotland.com, or
visithighlands.com

4 For something different

Terre à Terre, Brighton,
East Sussex
Amanda Powley and Philip
Taylor have pioneered a new
approach to vegetarian
cooking based on
imaginative combinations
of top-notch ingredients and
have won several awards as
a result. Inspired by recipes
from all over the world, their
menus change with the
seasons and are almost as
much fun to read as they
are to eat – with dishes such
as Ruby Tang Thang, Fancy
Nancy and Black Bean
Cellophane Frisbee. There

is a great children's menu
too, featuring favourites
such as Teeny Weeny
Linguine and Eggy Bread.
INFO 01273 729051
terreaterre.co.uk
STAY In Brighton 0300 300
0088 visitbrighton.com

5 For a chippy with an edge

Rick Stein's Fish & Chips,
Falmouth, Cornwall
The latest addition to Rick
Stein's stable – and the only
one outside Padstow, so far
– this is a jolly place within
metres of Falmouth's deep
water harbour. Padstow
favourites, such as battered
Icelandic cod fried in beef
dripping, are still on the
menu, but new additions
include charcoal-roasted
fish with thyme, parsley and
chilli. A horseshoe-shaped
seafood bar on the
mezzanine level serves River
Fowey oysters and other
fishy specials. The takeaway
and restaurant is three times
the size of Stein's original
restaurant in Padstow, with
white-tiled walls and
wooden bench seating;
expect an informal buzz
and watch out for queues,
as there's no booking.

Terre à Terre, Brighton, East Sussex

INFO Central reservations (for seafood bar only) 01841 532700 rickstein.com
STAY In Falmouth or nearby villages 01872 322900 visitcornwall.com

6 For a groovy vibe

Beach House, Shoreham-by-Sea, East Sussex
Chef Andrew Freeman has scoured the South Downs for the best producers to supply his café/bar/deli, which opened in 2009. His seasonal menus are based on free-range meat, wild game and organic vegetables plus the best of the daily catch from local fishermen. By day it's a laid-back café and deli; by night it's a restaurant, cocktail bar and live music venue, showcasing south-coast talent. Close to the Adur Estuary; the beach is a short stroll away.
INFO 01273 440902 beachhouseshoreham.co.uk
STAY In Shoreham-by-Sea or nearby Brighton 0300 300 0088 visitbrighton.com

7 For funky design

Urban Reef, Boscombe, near Bournemouth, Dorset
The team behind Bournemouth's hip Urban Beach hotel has taken up residence on the promenade of Boscombe's regenerated seafront overlooking the Boscombe surf reef. The result is a stylish restaurant, café, deli and bar serving skilfully cooked food. From three-course meals to burgers and chips, the influences range from Thailand to New England, with a commitment to fresh, local, seasonal produce. The vibe is cool and contemporary, with Formica tabletops and leather banquettes lending a fifties flavour, and you can come

Right: Freshly grilled sardines

Urban Reef, Boscombe, Dorset

in jeans or come in a suit – anything goes. Triple height picture windows give everyone a sea view.
INFO 01202 443960 urbanreef.com
STAY in Boscombe or Bournemouth 0845 051 1700 bournemouth.co.uk

8 For modern British

The Neptune, Old Hunstanton, Norfolk
You can't see the sea from The Neptune but it's only an eight-minute walk to Hunstanton's seafront with donkey rides and wooden chalets. Chef and co-owner Kevin Mangeolles has applied modern British inventiveness to local ingredients, with dishes such as butter-poached Brancaster lobster with star anise cream and pea purée, and Ballotine of mackerel, compressed watermelon, crab and horseradish salad. The mood is smart, neutral and intimate, with wood floors, white tablecloths and Lloyd Loom chairs seating 24 diners. There are comfortable rooms upstairs if you want to stay over.
INFO 01485 532122 theneptune.co.uk
STAY At The Neptune or elsewhere in Old Hunstanton 01485 532610 visitwestnorfolk.com, or norfolkcoast.co.uk

9 For beachside chic

The Cary Arms, Babbacombe, Devon
Walkers on the South West Coast Path can take a stylish pit stop in this renovated inn-cum-boutique hotel, owned by the de Savarys.

The Jetty, Christchurch, Dorset

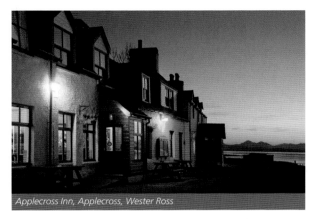
Applecross Inn, Applecross, Wester Ross

The food is seaside gastro pub-style, using fresh Devon produce: think Brixham crab salad with home-baked granary bread, and spiced apple crumble pie with Devon clotted cream, and you can wash it down with local ales and West Country cider. The Cary Arms has Riviera charm when it's sunny, and cosy comfort with log burning stoves when it's blustery, so it's a good all-year-rounder. Muddy boots and soggy dogs are heartily welcomed. There are eight rooms, two of which are dog-friendly. INFO 01803 327110 caryarms.co.uk STAY At The Cary Arms, or elsewhere in Babbacombe or nearby Shaldon 01803 211211 englishriviera.co.uk

10 For North Sea charm

Latimers Seafood Deli and Café, Whitburn, Tyne & Wear

The café at this award-winning fish shop on the Tynemouth to Sunderland coast path opened in mid 2009 and its bright, spacious feel, with a terrace facing Whitburn beach and the North Sea beyond, has proved popular with locals and visitors alike. There is a huge picture window, so even if the day is grey you can still savour the view. Owner Robert Latimer meets local boats every night to pick up the best of the catch and his wife Ailsa turns it into a daily changing selection of simple seafood classics: crab sandwiches, fruits de mer platters and home-made fish soup. There are always proper home-made cakes too. INFO 0191 529 2200 latimers.com STAY In Whitburn or nearby Seaham 0191 553 2000 visitsunderland.com

11 For a firm favourite

Porthminster Café, St Ives, Cornwall

Readers of coast Magazine love this relaxed, friendly café so much, they voted it best coastal café, pub or restaurant in the coast Awards 2010, runner-up in 2009 and joint winner in 2008! It's appreciated not only for its high standard of service and its culinary excellence, but also for its concern for sustainability and affordability. It even has its own vegetable, herb and salad garden with produce from it appearing daily on the menu. Sitting right on one of the cleanest beaches in the south-west, it is open from breakfast right through to dinner: expect local produce cooked with a Mediterranean/fusion bent, great Italian coffee, gorgeous patisserie and plenty of choice.

INFO 01736 795352
porthminstercafe.co.uk
STAY In St Ives or nearby Zennor 01872 322900
visitcornwall.com

12 For award-winning food

The Wee Restaurant, North Queensferry, Fife

A tiny restaurant with a huge reputation, The Wee features fine French cooking that has earned it a Michelin mention, using seasonal, local produce, including fish landed up the coast at Anstruther, along with weekly-changing dishes, such as mussels with bacon, basil, pine nuts and Parmesan; roast venison loin with mustard, celeriac cream and sage gnocchi; and baked chocolate fondant. Family-owned and run by Craig and Vikki Wood, it has a relaxed, unfussy mood, with dark wooden tables and whitewashed walls hung with work by local artists. Ask for the window table – it overlooks the mighty Forth Road Bridge that links the old-fashioned fishing village with Edinburgh, its sophisticated city neighbour.

INFO 01383 616263
theweerestaurant.co.uk
STAY In Queensferry or nearby Kirkcaldy
01592 267775
visitfife.com

13 For quayside cocktails

The Jetty, Christchurch, Dorset

Perched on the edge of Mudeford Quay, The Jetty restaurant occupies a state-of-the-art eco-building in the grounds of Christchurch Harbour Hotel. Inside is all minimalist charm with wooden floors, uncluttered wooden tables, warm lighting and generous views out over the harbour through walls of glass. Michelin-starred chef Alex Aitken heads up the team at the Restaurant, Bar and Grill, with a menu featuring fresh fish landed daily from Mudeford Quay, local oysters, shrimps and lobster and grills cooked in The Jetty's charcoal oven. Enjoy a drink or two on the waterside terrace if the weather is fine – they serve a very good cocktail.

INFO 01202 400950
thejetty.co.uk
STAY In Christchurch or nearby Bournemouth
01202 471780
visitchristchurch.info

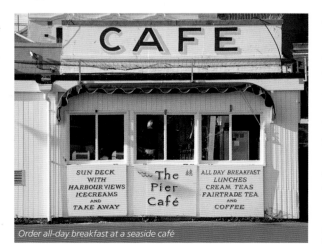

Order all-day breakfast at a seaside café

Right: Unbeatable – fresh, locally caught seafood

Edible seaweed

As well as providing a diverse habitat for shore life, the colourful range of seaweeds on the British coast can make a tasty addition to your dinner plate, so look out for some of these beauties while

Dulse
Palmaria palmata

DISTINGUISHING MARKS A red seaweed with flat, straight fronds that branch out to around 30cm. It's often found bunched together as its spores ('seeds') do not travel far from the parent plant.

WHERE TO SPOT Attached to rocks or other large seaweeds on lower shores around the UK; except sandy parts of the east coast.

GOOD EATING? Delicious eaten fresh and raw, simply washed in fresh water to reduce saltiness – or it can be baked or fried.

Sea Lettuce
Ulva lactuca

DISTINGUISHING MARKS Usually only a few centimetres wide, it has a bright green, leaf-like form that looks a little like it could grow into a cos lettuce.

WHERE TO SPOT On rocky coasts around the UK. It's very common in the middle of the shore.

GOOD EATING? Like lettuce, it's best eaten directly after picking, giving a salty tang but not a lot of flavour.

Alaria
Alaria esculenta

DISTINGUISHING MARKS A rib-like stem runs along the middle of a long (often 2m or more), wavy frond. This olive-green to brown-coloured kelp is a little less solid and rubbery than most other kelps.

WHERE TO SPOT Usually around, or just below, the low water mark on northern and western coasts.

GOOD EATING? The mid rib can be blanched or steamed, and is similar to artichoke or cardoons.

you're on your weekend travels. Spring is the perfect time to harvest, as seaweed is at its best when growing (stranded fronds decay very quickly). Never uproot a seaweed; don't take huge quantities; and, if you're in any doubt about water quality, give harvesting your own a miss and buy from a responsible specialist supplier instead.

Carrageen
Chondrus crispus

DISTINGUISHING MARKS Dark red, almost purple, with short fronds that quickly dry with a salty crust when out of water. It can grow up to 25cm but is usually smaller.

WHERE TO SPOT All around the UK, except in sandy parts of the east coast.

GOOD EATING? It's one of the most commonly eaten seaweeds, but is usually found in prepared foods – its 'agar jelly' helps thicken desserts like ice-cream and milkshakes, and processed meat and beer.

Laver
Porphyra umbilicalis

DISTINGUISHING MARKS Rather flat and purple in colour, this forms a slippery sheet on rocks when exposed to air by the tide. It doesn't look very appetising and is perhaps best obtained from farmed sources.

WHERE TO SPOT On rocky coasts around the UK.

GOOD EATING? Cooked with vegetables or bacon and seasoned, it makes great eating as 'laverbread' or other foods. Dried, it is highly regarded in Japan and called nori, often used to wrap sushi or as a seasoning.

Red Rags
Dilsea carnosa

DISTINGUISHING MARKS Similar to dulse, but with more numerous, smaller spoon-shaped fronds that can look torn and ragged.

WHERE TO SPOT Attached to rocks on lower shores around the UK, except sandy east coasts.

GOOD EATING? Although its raggedy appearance looks unappetising, it's much the same as dulse in both taste and texture.

Weekends for ice-cream and afternoon tea

That fine British custom of taking tea is experiencing a welcome revival, and where better to enjoy it than in an elegant seaside hotel or beachside café? Crisp white tablecloths, vintage china, scones with clotted cream and a sea view should all be on the menu. And if you're after a knickerbocker glory or a banana split, a traditional ice-cream parlour – boasting its original 1950s décor – is the perfect place to enjoy one. You can always walk off some of the calories with a stroll along the beach afterwards…

This page: Hocking's ice-cream van at Westward Ho!, Devon

1 For panoramic sea views

Idle Rocks Hotel,
St Mawes, Cornwall

Perched on the edge of the harbour wall in the fishing village of St Mawes – on the outermost tip of the Roseland Peninsula – Idle Rocks is in an enviable spot. Traditional Cornish cream tea is served on the terrace, perfect for watching the action float by in the harbour. If you fancy staying for dinner, try the hotel's acclaimed Water's Edge restaurant which serves locally caught crab and lobster.

INFO Idle Rocks Hotel 0800 005 3901 or 01326 270771 idlerocks.co.uk

STAY In St Mawes or nearby Towan Beach 01326 270440 (St Mawes Tourist Information) visitcornwall.com

2 For fifties retro

Harbour Bar,
Scarborough, North Yorkshire

Virtually unchanged since it opened in 1945, Harbour Bar's interior is a tribute to the American soda parlour, with its red leatherette banquettes, neon signs, gleaming chrome and riot of yellow and white Formica. Run by the Alonzi family, it's famed for its classic ice-cream dishes, especially knickerbocker glories. Open daily; closed Wednesday in winter and all November.

INFO Harbour Bar 01723 373662, or classiccafes.co.uk

Idle Rocks Hotel, St Mawes, Cornwall

STAY In Scarborough or nearby Filey 01723 383636 discoveryorkshirecoast.com

3 For sundae treats
Morelli's, Broadstairs, Kent

With its 1950s interior still intact, Morelli's is a gem. Visitors sit on pink vinyl banquettes or Lloyd Loom chairs, there's an Italian water fountain embellished with colourful artificial flowers, and sundaes are served in hand-blown glasses with elegant parfait spoons. The Morelli family has made ice-cream for five generations since Guiseppe Morelli left his small village near Naples in 1907 and began selling his home-made ice-cream by bicycle in Scotland. Morelli's, Broadstairs was opened in 1932. All ice-cream is still made on the premises from fresh double cream, sugar, eggs and milk – chocolate nut sundae is their bestseller but the family make all sorts, including seasonal mince pie and Christmas pudding flavours. Belvidere Place, nearby, is a great place to stay: an eccentric boutique hotel.

Harbour Bar, Scarborough, North Yorkshire

INFO 01843 862500 morellis.com
STAY Belvidere Place 01843 579850 belvidereplace.co.uk, or elsewhere in Broadstairs 01843 577577 visitthanet.co.uk

4 For Italian sundaes
Notarianni Ice Cream, Blackpool, Lancashire

Italian immigrant Luigi Notarianni sold his first ice-cream in Scotland at the turn of the last century, then moved to Blackpool where the family ice-cream parlour has sold cornets and sundaes to holidaymakers ever since. Good, old-fashioned vanilla ice-cream is the order of the day here, along with all the classic sundaes including peach melbas, knickerbocker glories, banana splits and the Notarianni, which features the colours of Italy with kiwi fruit and strawberries.
INFO 01253 342510 notarianniicecreamblackpool. co.uk
STAY In Blackpool or nearby Lytham 01253 478222 visitblackpool.com

5 For the classic beach café
The Dennis Café, Tenby, Pembrokeshire

It's not swish but it's charming. The old-fashioned booths of this family-run café on St Julian's Terrace,

Castle Beach are always filled with coast-lovers, looking out to sea beside cups of tea, coffee and slices of Welsh cake and apple pie. Full Welsh breakfast, burgers and veggie options are available too. Open from April to late October.

INFO The Dennis Café 01834 842298

STAY In Tenby or nearby Amroth 01834 842402 visitpembrokeshire.com

6 For wicked flavours

Fusciardi's Ice Cream, Tea & Coffee Lounge, Eastbourne, East Sussex

This delightful, small family-run parlour has been serving Italian ice-cream here since

Left: Morelli's, Broadstairs, Kent

1967. To the east of the pier, on the seafront in Marine Parade, it has a suitably retro interior, with Formica tables and a liberal use of gold paint. Ice-cream is made on the premises and so they usually experiment with different flavours every week. Favourites include pistachio and a widely rated honeycomb.

INFO Fusciardi's 01323 722128

STAY In Eastbourne or nearby Bexhill 0871 663 0031 visiteastbourne.com

7 For home-made cake

Naze Links Café, Walton-on-the-Naze, Essex

Allow loitering time at this friendly, no-frills seaside café

as you try to choose between Barbara and Rodney Russell's collection of tempting home-baked cakes, scones and pies. Should it be Rodney's renowned bread pudding or Barbara's coffee cake? The deep-filled apple pie or a fruit scone? Check out the blackboard for the day's specials. Bacon rolls, jacket potatoes and ploughman's are on offer too, as well as fresh sandwiches and rolls, ideal for taking with you on a beach walk. The café, on Old Hall Lane, is near the landmark 86-feet-high octagonal Naze Tower and is open every day in summer and on winter weekends.

INFO Naze Links Café 07885 385171

Skoon Art Café, Isle of Harris, Outer Hebrides

STAY In Walton-on-the-Naze or nearby Clacton-on-Sea 01255 675542 or 01255 686633 essex-sunshine-coast.org.uk

8 For picture-postcard views

Soar Mill Cove Hotel, Salcombe, Devon

Gaze up the steep, gorse-covered valley from the sheltered sandy bay of Soar Mill Cove and you'll see this single-storey, modernist hotel, in a fold of National Trust land. Many of its rooms, including the lounge where afternoon tea is served, have expansive views of the coast and it is noted for its home-made scones, tea cakes and Dundee cake. Closed from Christmas to mid-February. INFO Soar Mill Cove Hotel 01548 561566 soarmillcove.co.uk STAY In Salcombe or nearby Hope Cove 01548 843927 salcombeinformation.co.uk

9 For contemporary chic

Ocean Bay, Swanage, Dorset

If it weren't for its spectacular location on Swanage North Beach, this quayside restaurant's super-cool indigo and cream décor would make it feel like a bar or club. Dorset cream teas are served inside or on the terrace overlooking the water, as are cocktails and an extensive menu of local produce with a modern twist. If you prefer to arrive by water, you'll be pleased to know that guests have use of 12 moorings. INFO 01929 422222 oceanbayrestaurant.com STAY In Swanage or nearby Studland 01929 422885 visitswanageandpurbeck. co.uk

10 For log fires and gentility

Sea Marge Hotel, Overstrand, Norfolk

With mock Tudor gables, oak panelling and latticed windows, this Grade II-listed house in High Street looks like the setting for a period drama. It was built in 1908 for banker Sir Edgar Speyer, as a seaside residence for his family and friends. When it opened as a hotel in 1935, Winston Churchill was among the first A-list guests. Traditional Norfolk cream teas are served in the Winston Room, with views of the lawns and sea beyond. INFO 01263 579579 seamargehotel.co.uk STAY At the hotel, elsewhere in Overstrand or nearby Cromer 0871 200 3071 visitnorthnorfolk.com

11 For escape artists

Skoon Art Café, Isle of Harris, Outer Hebrides

Perched high on rocky coastline and looking across the sea to Skye, this tiny art gallery-café feels like it is at the edge of the world. Along with its chilled atmosphere, you will enjoy its wide selection of teas, freshly ground coffee, delicious cakes and oil paintings of the local coastline by co-owner Andrew John Craig. See website for opening times. INFO 01859 530268 skoon.com STAY In Tarbert, Isle of Harris 0845 2255121 visitscotland.com

Right: Hocking's Ice-cream, Westward Ho!, Devon

Weekends for foodie treats

We are fast beginning to realise just what a wealth of fantastic fish and seafood we have at our disposal and how to enjoy it. Our fish markets are bursting with fresh sea treats and the health benefits of eating fish are well-known. Festivals celebrating this rich harvest – whether it's of oysters, scallops or herrings – are springing up all over the place. Read on for our recommended round-up, and if you're unsure of the best ways to cook fish or want to notch up your seafood skills, why not go on a course?

This page: Taking to the sand for a beach barbecue

1 For the freshest oysters

Whitstable Oyster Festival, Whitstable, Kent

Whitstable celebrates the heritage of its favourite bivalve mollusc at this annual festival each July, where you can also enjoy other epicurean delights and the town's particular brand of eccentric festival atmosphere. It incorporates traditional elements, such as a blessing of the sea by the clergy and a costumed parade delivering oysters through the town. It also embraces such activities as samba bands, street theatre and music and dancing of all sorts. Scour the 50+ stalls for tasty food and drink including delicious, juicy oysters and freshly landed fish, along with beer made with Kentish hops and other delights from the nearby Garden of England. If you've the stomach for it, go and watch (or enter?) the highly competitive oyster eating challenge. INFO 01227 862066 whitstableoysterfestival.com STAY In Whitstable or nearby Herne Bay 01227 378100 (Whitstable and Herne Bay Tourist Information) canterbury.co.uk

2 For master chefs

The Dorset Seafood Festival, Weymouth, Dorset

Weymouth is a proper, old-fashioned British seaside town. In summer, fairground rides and donkeys line its front, and families brush sand from their feet as they queue for fish and chips. Come July, things get grander with the Dorset Seafood Festival. Celeb chefs such as Mark Hix and

Oyster Festival, Whitstable, Kent

Mat Follas bring their piscine knowledge to the old harbour, where they will prepare and cook local produce. Other events include wine tastings and displays plus the Dorset Young Seafood Masterchef Competition. Wandering through the 50+ stalls, sampling Dorset's finest fish will cost you nothing although there may be too many temptations to resist buying some foodie delights. There are also live performances from the best bands on Weymouth's vibrant music scene. Check date on website.
INFO 01305 785747 visitweymouth.co.uk or dorsetseafood.co.uk
STAY In Weymouth 01305 785747 visitweymouth.co.uk

Herring Festival, Clovelly, Devon

3 For sampling scallops

Rye Bay Scallop Week, Rye, East Sussex
One of the medieval Cinque Ports, Rye was once surrounded on three sides by the sea but the coast has gradually silted up since the 16th century, leaving the town lying two miles from open water. It still maintains a 20-strong fishing fleet, however, which plays a pivotal role in the annual Rye Bay Scallop Week (including two weekends), held in February. See website for dates/times. Fans of this juicy bivalve will be in their element: the usual events include chances to watch them being prepared and cooked, taste them (of course!), enjoy them in a four-course lunch, even watch them being barrowed through the narrow streets in the 'What a Load of Scallops' race, organised by The Ship Inn. Fun and flavour for all.

Camber Sands is a bus hop away, so you can walk it all off afterwards.
INFO ryebayscallops.co.uk
STAY 01797 229049
visitrye.co.uk, or
ryebayscallops.co.uk

4 For Fal oysters

Falmouth Oyster Festival, Falmouth, Cornwall
For 14 years, the start of each oyster season in October has been celebrated by the four-day Falmouth Oyster Festival, with marquees erected on Discovery Quay, stalls full of Cornish produce and a programme of events celebrating the diversity and quality of Cornish seafood. Oysters are gathered according to traditional methods of harvesting using only sail and oar, and they are so fresh, the whole marquee smells of the sea. Events include a cookery masterclass from a celebrity chef, demonstrations by top local chefs, live music, sea shanties, a Grand Parade, working boat race, an oyster shucking competition and Oyster Ball.
INFO falmouthoysterfestival.co.uk

STAY In Falmouth or Penryn
01326 312300
discoverfalmouth.co.uk

5 For hot stuff

South Devon Chilli Farm, Loddiswell, Kingsbridge, Devon
Jason Nickels and Steve Waters swapped computers for polytunnels when they gave up IT jobs to grow chillies eight years ago. They now grow more than 10,000 chilli plants a year and sell more than 20 fresh and dried varieties, as well as home-made sauces, jams and jellies ranging from warm to incendiary. The mild climate and late frosts are particularly beneficial and fresh chillies are harvested between July and November. Wander among the chilli plants, sample all the sauces, preserves and chocolate (their bestseller) and take away chilli seedlings, plants and seeds.
INFO 01548 550782
southdevonchillifarm.co.uk
STAY In Kingsbridge or Bigbury-on-Sea
01548 853195
kingsbridgeinfo.co.uk

6 For seafood cookery

Padstow Seafood School, Padstow, Cornwall
At Rick Stein's school you can get to grips with all the basics of cooking fish in an enjoyable day of demonstrations and hands-on cooking broken up by the important bit – lunch – where you get to enjoy the fruits of your labours. The atmosphere is relaxed and the school has windows overlooking the harbour so it's a pleasant place to spend a day, learning something new and useful. Original Fish and Shellfish Cookery covers the techniques needed for impressive fish dishes; Classic Seafood Dishes concentrates on time-honoured recipes such as fish soup with rouille. Other courses cover Italian, French and Far Eastern fish cookery.
INFO 01841 532700
rickstein.com
STAY In Padstow or nearby Wadebridge 01841 533 449
padstowlive.com

Right: Fresh-cooked seafood, River Cottage, Devon

7 For herrings

Herring Festival, Clovelly, Devon

There's kippers galore at Clovelly's Herring Festival in November. Known affectionately by fishermen as 'the silver darlings' of the sea, herring were once a mainstay of this impossibly pretty Devon fishing village. Now, on this one weekend in November (check website for date and times) you can trundle down its steep, cobbled main street to the harbour and learn about the history of the once great herring industry. The event, which is held in support of sustainable traditional fishing, includes 'Kipperland', smoking kippers and bloaters; demonstrations of traditional crafts including net making and flax processing, plus herring specialities, cider, wine and shanty singing. Stay in one of Clovelly's two hotels or a local B&B or self-catering.
INFO 01237 431781 clovelly.co.uk
STAY 01237 431781 clovelly.co.uk, or visitdevon.co.uk

8 For brushing up skills

The Cookery School at Dunbrody Country House Hotel, County Wexford
Set in 300 acres of dreamy parkland on the Hook Peninsula on Ireland's southern coast, this Georgian manor house hotel is an elegant place to learn how to whip up fine food using local ingredients, at the cooking school adjoining the hotel. One-day courses might take in seafood and shellfish, great family food, easy entertaining or one-pot wonders. They have all been devised by Irish celebrity chef Kevin Dundon, who owns Dunbrody. The emphasis is on freshness and seasonality of locally sourced ingredients and using these to achieve great dishes without the worry of overly complicated recipes.
INFO Irish Tourist Information 08000 397000 discoverireland.com
STAY At Dunbrody Country House Hotel 00 353 51 389 600 dunbrodyhouse.com

9 For pungent fare

The Isle of Wight Garlic Festival, Sandown, Isle of Wight
Garlic sausages, bread, beer, even fudge and ice-cream… you name it, you can find it at the now internationally renowned Isle of Wight Garlic Festival, which is held to celebrate the fact that the

Isle of Wight Garlic Festival

island is the number one garlic growing region in the UK (at The Garlic Farm, in Newchurch). The organisers describe it as 'a curious mix of late sixties pop festival ambience, country fair and garlic cuisine'. There's a huge garlic tent, of course, but you'll also find a great number of other foodstuffs the island is good at, from award-winning local lamb, beef, pork and poultry to dairy products, fruit, vegetables and juices.

INFO 01983 614612 garlic-festival.co.uk. The Garlic Farm 01983 865378 thegarlicfarm.co.uk STAY In Sandown or nearby Bembridge 01983 813813 islandbreaks.co.uk

10 Best for family cooking

Manna from Devon, Kingswear, Devon
Relaxed, hands-on cooking classes take place in the purpose-built cookery school with B&B at Fir Mount House – a Victorian property

overlooking the River Dart in Kingswear, South Hams. Run by chef, food writer and broadcaster Holly Jones and her husband David, the school offers a family- and child-friendly timetable with classes such as Family Mediterranean and Family Barbecue. Fabulous Fish is a one-day course, giving you the chance to scale, gut, fillet and clean fish (if you want to!) and then go on to prepare a number of different dishes. This includes a late lunch to

Oyster Festival, Falmouth, Cornwall

taste and discuss what you've prepared.

INFO 01803 752943 mannafromdevon.com STAY At Manna from Devon's Fir Mount House B&B, elsewhere in Kingswear or nearby Dartmouth 01803 834224 discoverdartmouth.com

11 For foraging skills

River Cottage, Axminster, Devon

Although this one-day course is often held on a Thursday rather than on a Saturday or Sunday, you might just want to lengthen your weekend in order to take it in. John Wright, foraging expert and author of the River Cottage Handbook, *Edible Seashore*, takes a small group along the Jurassic coastline in search of shellfish and a variety of edible seaweeds and vegetation such as sea beet and sea radish.

Then it's back to River Cottage HQ where John and the River Cottage team will demonstrate recipes based on typical seashore finds, hopefully including your morning's haul, which you'll get to eat later on. A late lunch is included, as well as a copy of *Edible Seashore*. Other day courses include Fish Skills and Cookery and A Day of Meat Curing and Smoking.

INFO 01297 630 302 rivercottage.net STAY In Axminster or nearby Lyme Regis 01297 442138 lymeregis.org

Right: Landing the catch at the Oyster Festival, Whitstable, Kent

South Devon Chilli Farm, Kingsbridge, Devon

Weekends for glam camping

There's something both romantic and intrepid about camping by the sea: what could be better than waking up to the sound of the ocean and the rattle of a kettle on the stove? But if you have been put off by the thought of roughing it, the new, more luxurious campsites could be the answer. Offering smart facilities – from geodesic domes and Romany caravans to tipis and Mongolian yurts – they take the strain out of preparation and set-up, leaving you to enjoy all the best bits of camping under the stars.

This page: Yurt at Lombard Farm, Fowey Cornwall

1 For romantic seclusion

Romany Caravan & Cabin, Rhydlewis, Ceredigion
Tucked away in an acre of riverside meadow a little inland from the west Wales coast, Under The Thatch's bow-topped caravan enjoys a picturesque location. Built in 1924, it has a double bed and potbelly stove, plus discreet plug sockets and electric lighting so you can snuggle up in bed and watch DVDs on your laptop if you want to. The Cabin, nearby, has a kitchen, shower room and veranda, but meals can also be enjoyed at the campfire and picnic bench down by the water's edge, so you watch the brown trout swimming by. Available all year.

INFO Cardigan Tourist Information 01239 613230 tourism.ceredigion.gov.uk
STAY Under The Thatch 01239 851410 underthethatch.co.uk

2 For wooden wigwams

Pot-a-Doodle Do Wigwam Village, Scremerston, Northumberland
Each of the 20 quirky tent-shaped cabins – known as wooden wigwams – comes complete with spectacular views of Holy Island, the Farne Islands and Bamburgh Castle. You can be at one with nature here yet still enjoy full insulation, comfy mattresses, heating and electricity. There's even a fridge. And with a licensed shop, café/bistro and barbecue hut on site, the weather can't spoil the fun. Each wigwam sleeps five and there are three canvas yurts, too; small, for five, or large, for eight people. Mid-February–December.

INFO Berwick-upon-Tweed Tourist Information 01289 330733

Romany Caravan, Rhydlewis, Ceredigion

Tipis at Ogmore by Sea, Glamorgan

visitnorthumberland.com
STAY Pot-a-Doodle Do
01289 307107
northumbrianwigwams.com

3 For Pocahontas wannabes

Cornish Tipi Holidays, Tregildrans Quarry, St Kew, Cornwall
Established in 1997, this woodland tipi village is set around a spring-fed lake two miles inland from the north coast of Cornwall. Each tipi – available in three sizes – is made of cotton canvas on a framework of locally sourced wooden lodge poles and is more than 18 feet tall. There are Turkish rugs on the ground, along with lanterns, a camp stove and coolbox. Within a short drive you can buy fresh mackerel, scallops and crab at Port Isaac or go sea kayaking at Port Quin. April–October; short breaks available in low and mid-season.
INFO 01872 322900
visitcornwall.com
STAY 01208 880781
cornishtipiholidays.co.uk

4 For getting back to nature

Lunsford Farm, Pett, Hastings, East Sussex
In a clearing at the edge of a small copse, these 'tents' may have thick canvas roofing, but hidden beneath are solid wooden floors, three separate sleeping areas and traditional furnishings, along with a well-equipped kitchen and bedding. They sleep six and there's even room for a wooden table and chairs inside, under cover. Lunsford Farm has

been designated a Site of Special Scientific Interest (SSSI), as it forms part of the Old Saxon shoreline, and you can walk down to the beach, just ten minutes away. There is also a campfire, where you can toast marshmallows. April–October.

INFO Hastings Tourist Information 01424 451111 visit1066country.com
STAY Feather Down Farms 01420 80804 featherdownfarm.co.uk

5 For shoreline sunsets

Mill Haven Place, Talbenny, Pembrokeshire
Just a mile from the coast Award-winning Pembrokeshire Coast Path, this eco-campsite, with four ready-pitched and fully furnished yurts, is on a six-acre organic smallholding, overlooking the Irish Sea. On site are eco-compost toilets and a shower block, and all yurts come with double bed, hand-made woodburning stoves, two sofabed chairs and a covered, fully equipped outside kitchen, so you can experience real comfort while getting back to nature.

Each yurt sleeps up to five. There are also a few pitches for a caravan, tent or motorhome, if you want to bring your own. May–October; weekends in the low season.
INFO 01437 7763110 visitpembrokeshire.com
STAY 01437 781633 millhavenplace.co.uk

6 For green luxe

The Apple Farm at Afton Park, Freshwater Bay, Isle of Wight
Solar-powered lights, candle lanterns and wood from sustainable woodland – this tranquil site on the west coast of the Isle of Wight is all about being eco-friendly. Luxury hasn't suffered, though, as all five yurts are kitted out just like a holiday cottage – there's even one with a four-poster bed. The site is level and leafy and it's less than ten minutes from the beach, with plenty of good walking and cycling on the doorstep. You can buy provisions, many of them locally produced, from the on-site shop and there is a café – The Apple Tree Café – specialising in organic produce. April–October.

INFO IoW Tourist Information 01983 813813 islandbreaks.co.uk
STAY The Apple Farm 07802 678591 thereallygreenholiday company. com

7 For quirky beauty

Henry's Campsite, Helston, Cornwall
Not so much glam as quirky and individual, regulars speak highly of this campsite – they love it. Much hard work on the part of owners Jo and Ron and Ron's father, the eponymous Henry, has gone into making it what it is. They run it the way they want to run it and people come back year after year to enjoy its many charms. One happy camper described it as a 'sub-tropical, sculptural, artistic masterpiece'! It is the most southerly in Britain, not far from the coastal path, so there is great walking to be had in all directions. If you're happy to go with the flow, are looking for something a little bit out of the ordinary and don't mind your loos and showers being in a unisex block, this is the place

Right: Lunsford Farm, Pett, Hastings, East Sussex

for you. Open all year.
INFO 01872 322900
visitcornwall.com
STAY 01326 290596
henryscampsite.co.uk

8 For would-be Sioux

Tipis at Ogmore by Sea, Glamorgan Heritage Coast

There'll be plenty of time for bonding round the campfire here as you can light a fire either outside or in (there's a special 'chimney' to vent the smoke). Each of the three large tipis sleeps up to eight. Bring your own sleeping bags and you can lay your head down on a suspended wooden floor on a base of coir matting and rugs. They're sited a mile and a half from the large sandy beach at Ogmore by Sea, part of the Heritage Coast, and when you lift your flap in the morning you'll be looking at the 12th century Ogmore Castle ruins across the field. A thatched tea room and a local pub are nearby, as are toilet and shower facilities and beach riding. March–September.
INFO 08708 300 306
visitwales.co.uk or 01656 654906 visitbridgend.com.
Ogmore Farm Riding
01656 880856
rideonthebeach.co.uk
STAY 01656 880008
tipiwales.co.uk

9 For breathing space

Lombard Farm, Fowey, Cornwall

If it's bags of space you're after, book into this six-metre-diameter yurt, located about three miles from the sea, near Fowey. Built using locally grown, steam-bent ash, the yurt sleeps five so it's great for families or a

Vintage Vacations, Ashey, Isle of Wight

group of friends. There is one double bed and three single futons and there's space to cook on the two-ring gas cooker and grill, and to eat at a solid wooden table with seating. The yurt is tucked away behind mature trees, with views over a meadow towards the River Fowey. An outdoor barbecue is at your disposal, and there's also use of a wooden hot tub and shared 'Link' building with Wi-Fi, solar showers, fridge, microwave, toaster etc. April–October.
INFO Fowey Tourist Information 01726 833616 fowey.co.uk
STAY 01726 870844 adventurecornwall.co.uk

10 For a pleasure dome

Fforest by the Sea, Manorafon, Ceredigion
Looking like space capsules, these six-metre-diameter geodesic domes take all the best bits of staying in a hotel to the outdoors. Welsh wool blankets and cushions cosy up the interiors, and breakfast is served in a converted stable block. Next to Penbryn beach, the camp also has a

fire pit and cedar barrel sauna. The domes sleep four adults or two adults and two to three children. There are also tunnel style tents from the Netherlands, which sleep the same numbers. March–October. Winter breaks available.
INFO Cardigan Tourist Information 01239 613230 tourism.ceredigion.gov.uk
STAY Manorafon 01239 623633 coldatnight.co.uk

11 For American retro

Vintage Vacations, Ashey, Isle of Wight
Dating from the 1940s to the 1960s, these refurbished American Airstream caravans moved to a new site in 2010 at Hazlegrove Farm, near Ryde. All ten have been restored and have authentic retro furnishings with crocheted bedspreads and vintage board games, and, as well as the on-board hot shower, Vintage Vacations has also laid on a separate shower block and loos and a shop-in-a-shed. Holidaymakers are treated to a Babycham and cream tea on arrival. Sleeps two to six. April–October.

INFO IoW Tourist Information 01983 813813 islandbreaks.co.uk
STAY 07802 758113 vintagevacations.co.uk

12 For cosy comfort

Deepdale Farm, Burnham Deepdale, Norfolk
Scant light pollution offers the perfect opportunity for stargazing from Mongolian yurts at this eco-friendly campsite on the north Norfolk coast. All are furnished with futons and a wood-burning stove. There are tipis too, equipped with a faux-fur sleeping mat, chiminea and barbecue. And, for pet lovers, there is even a dog-friendly tipi. In the morning, you can look out over fields and woods on this fourth generation family farm between Hunstanton and Wells-Next-the-Sea. The tipis and yurts sleep from two to six. There are also open pitches if you prefer to bring your own tent or campervan. Open all year.
INFO Deepdale Visitor Information 01485 210256 brancasterstaithe.co.uk
STAY Deepdale Farm 01485 210256 deepdalebackpackers.co.uk

Pier fish

The attractions of piers are not just confined to their decks; what lies in the sea below is just as interesting. Mussels, limpets and seaweed become attached to the supports of piers and these attract

Tompot Blenny

Parablennius gattorugine

DISTINGUISHING MARKS
An appealing fish, which grows to around 30cm, and has distinctive 'eyebrows' above each eye, as well as an endearing facial expression.

WHERE TO SPOT In the south and west.

BEST PIERS TO SEE IT Swanage; Southend.

A CURIOUS THING A tompot will inhabit holes and crevices in pier legs, and guard its territory fearlessly.

Bass

Dicentrarchus labrax

DISTINGUISHING MARKS
A long and agile hunter of small fish that prowls amid the shallows. Grows to 80cm.

WHERE TO SPOT Most common in the south and west.

BEST PIERS TO SEE IT Torquay; Boscombe.

A CURIOUS THING Our bass breed in the Bay of Biscay. Sadly, they are fished while spawning and many dolphins are accidentally caught among them.

John Dory

Zeus faber

DISTINGUISHING MARKS
Face on, the John Dory looks like a narrow apparition but from the side, its craggy features, spiky fins and a big black spot on its side are unmistakable. Grows to 40cm in length.

WHERE TO SPOT Most abundant on Atlantic coasts.

BEST PIERS TO SEE IT Swanage; Bournemouth.

A CURIOUS THING It usually appears deceptively motionless, but can be very active when chasing prey – manoeuvring sideways and even upside down.

fish, which then come in to feed. You can spot various different species of fish just by peering over the edge of the pier. If you want to take a closer look, you'll need to put on a mask and snorkel – but it's worth just checking the local signage first, or asking a lifeguard whether it is safe to swim close to the pier's structure. Also watch out for fishermen casting their lines.

Coley (or Saithe)
Pollachius virens

DISTINGUISHING MARKS
Brownish, cod-like fish, which grows to 60cm and more. It has a distinctive single pale line along the side of its body.

WHERE TO SPOT May be found anywhere along the UK coast, but more common in the north and east.

BEST PIERS TO SEE IT Scarborough; Saltburn.

A CURIOUS THING It can grow to an enormous size – weighing over 20kg – though sadly few reach such proportions due to fishing.

Bib (or Pouting)
Trisopterus luscus

DISTINGUISHING MARKS
Cod-like fish but with a subtle banding down the body. It grows to around 50cm.

WHERE TO SPOT Common, especially on south and west coasts.

BEST PIERS TO SEE IT Bangor; Worthing.

A CURIOUS THING This shoaling fish happily swims among bathers and divers in shallow water.

Grey Mullet (Thick Lipped)
Chelon labrosus

DISTINGUISHING MARKS
A sleek, silvery fish with a torpedo shape. Up to 60cm and a fast swimmer. It often shelters among pier legs.

WHERE TO SPOT Southern coasts.

BEST PIERS TO SEE IT Mumbles; Teignmouth.

A CURIOUS THING It really does have 'lips' that graze on a diet of muddy algae.

Weekends for pier and lighthouse lovers

Steeped in romance and maritime history, piers and lighthouses hold an undeniable fascination for coast lovers. Quite apart from all the fun you can expect to have at the end of it, a pier's lure is that it allows you to take a stroll right out over the water, while in a lighthouse, you get the chance to climb high up into the air, offering you panoramic views all around. Either way, a visit to one will give you a whole new perspective on our shoreline. We have turned the spotlight on some of the riches these iconic seaside structures have to offer.

This page: South Stack Lighthouse, Holyhead, Anglesey

1 For thrills and spills

Blackpool South Pier, Lancashire

Tired of sitting in a deckchair? Then why not leave your stomach on the floor at Blackpool's South Pier while the rest of your body heads into the sky at 100mph? The Skyscreamer, a reverse bungee-jump, fires up to three people into the air, while in the Skycoaster, the thrill-seeker is hoisted 100 feet above the pier then dropped and swung out over the beach. For the less adventurous, there is the Storm Chaser (like a waltzer). Or the dodgems. Admission free, charges for rides vary.
INFO 01253 478222
visitblackpool.com
STAY In Blackpool or nearby Lytham 01253 478222
visitblackpool.com

2 For staying power

Saltburn Pier, Yorkshire

Poor Saltburn Pier has been buffeted and bashed in a series of mostly weather-related disasters over the years, losing its end more than once. The arrival of the railway in 1860 established Saltburn's future as a resort, but the 1,500-foot pier has proved disaster-prone, with its exposed northerly situation not helping. When it was threatened with demolition in the 1970s, locals fought to restore it, albeit in a truncated form – it is now just 681 feet long. Improvements include a pier head and ambitious lighting scheme (embracing the neighbouring cliff lift). Admission free.
INFO 01287 622528
Redcar-cleveland.gov.uk/leisure
STAY In Saltburn or nearby Whitby saltburnbysea.com

3 For organic grub

Souter Lighthouse, Seaham, County Durham

Around 11 miles north of Seaham is the iconically red-

Souter Lighthouse, Seaham, County Durham

and-white-stripe painted Souter Lighthouse. Now owned by the National Trust, it's worth a visit for its café alone, which serves organic produce grown in the gardens. It was a technological marvel when it was first opened in 1871 – the first lighthouse to use electricity. It stopped operating in 1988. Climb the 76 steps to the top and enjoy expansive views of Marsden Bay and beyond, where the notorious currents have claimed many ships. And when you're down on terra firma again, you can explore the Leas – a two-and-a-half-mile stretch of beach, cliff and grassland. INFO Souter Lighthouse 0191 529 3161 nationaltrust.org.uk STAY In Seaham or nearby Whitburn 0191 553 2000 visitsunderland.com

4 For southern belles

Lizard Lighthouse, Cornwall

If you're looking for insight into the life of a lighthouse keeper and the role of lighthouses in sea safety, the Lizard is the place to

Llandudno Pier, Conwy

come. The interactive visitor centre, which opened in 2009, is housed in the engine room and still features some of the original engines. The Lizard Peninsula is the most southerly point in mainland England and this wild coastline first had a lighthouse in 1619, while the present structure dates from 1752. There are two towers with six cottages in between, which are available for self-catering holidays. INFO Lizard Lighthouse 01326 290202 trinityhouse.co.uk STAY Lighthouse cottages 01326 240333 cornishcottagesonline.com, or elsewhere on the Lizard lizard-peninsula.co.uk

5 For catching fish

Deal Pier, Kent

The pier at Deal is a must for all fishermen. Anglers are welcomed by a huge statue of a man landing fish the size of sharks, before strolling along this stylish 1950s construction in search of smaller fry. But enthusiasts who don't get a bite won't go hungry. Grafted onto the original concrete structure is a bright, modern new café, designed by renowned architects Niall McLaughlin, who won a national award for architecture for the structure. Admission free; see dealpier.com website for fishing prices. INFO Deal Pier 01304 872448 dover.gov.uk/dealpier, or

01304 363815 dealpier.com
STAY In Deal or nearby
Sandwich 01304 369576
whitecliffscountry.org.uk

6 For strolls and sunsets

Clevedon Pier, Somerset
For a saunter and a
sensational sunset, head
to the end of Britain's most
elegant pier at Clevedon.
Built in 1869 on iron arches,
it seems to float above the
sea. An exotic-looking
pavilion provides views of
the Severn Estuary, its two

Left: Brighton Pier, East Sussex

bridges and Flat Holm and
Steep Holm islands. Time
your visit right and you can
enjoy a boat trip aboard
Waverley, the last sea-going
paddle steamer or the classic
cruise ship *Balmoral*.
INFO Clevedon Pier 01275
878846 clevedonpier.com
STAY In Clevedon or nearby
Weston-super-Mare 01934
426020 visitsomerset.co.uk

7 For a ride out to sea

Southend Pier, Essex
Southend needed Britain's
longest pier to be able to

land passengers from
steamers at low tide, and
at one and a third miles,
it is still the world's longest
pleasure pier. For the keen
walker, a brisk trot to the
end and back may seem
tempting, but, for the rest
of us, it might be more
pleasurable to 'let the train
take the strain'. In 1888
work began on an electric
railway, and today, the pier
is served by two diesel trains.
A fire wiped out the station
and pub in 2005 but there's
now a new station, a café
and one of the country's

Clevedon Pier, Somerset

busiest lifeboat stations.
INFO 01702 215620
southendpier.co.uk
STAY In Southend-on-Sea or
nearby Leigh-on-Sea 01702
618747 visitsouthend.co.uk

8 For architecture buffs

Llandudno Pier,
Llandudno, Conwy
Walking out onto the
Y-shaped pier at Llandudno,
which opened in 1877, is
like walking into an oriental
fantasy, with its elaborate
wrought ironwork and
curving roofs. But it's not a
homage to the Far East, just
the further east, because it
is the influence of the Prince
Regent's Brighton Pavilion
that's visible in the 'Indian
Gothic' architecture here. Its

striking looks have earned it
a place in TV period dramas,
such as *The Forsyte Saga*.
Admission free.
INFO Llandudno Tourist
Information 01492 577577
visitllandudno.org.uk
STAY In Llandudno or
nearby Conwy Llandudno
01492 577577
visitllandudno.org.uk

9 For a historic tale

Hook Lighthouse, County
Wexford
Dating from the 13th
century, Hook is one of
the oldest operational
lighthouses in the world and
was once manned by monks.
It's the only one in Ireland
open to the public and on a
clear day you can see whales
and Wales from its tower,

which marks the entrance
to Waterford Harbour. Its
construction is interesting
in itself – it's made of local
limestone and survives
almost intact, complete
with vaulted ceilings and an
original fireplace. There are
115 steps to the parapet
and your guide will tell you
its tale along the way. See
website for opening times.
INFO Hook Lighthouse
00 353 (0)51 397 054
hookheritage.ie
STAY In Hook or nearby
villages hooktourism.com,
or discoverireland.com

10 For traditional fairground fun

Brighton Pier, East Sussex
The end of Brighton Pier
boasts a collection of
fairground rides, including
a ghost train, a surviving
helter-skelter, dodgems and
the Wild River log flume.
At the heart of this is the
Palace of Fun, a modern,
domed structure on the site
of the old theatre, with slot
machines and arcade games,
whose tunes provide a blast
of nostalgia for holidays
past. Admission free.
INFO 01273 609361
brightonpier.co.uk

Llandudno Pier, Conwy

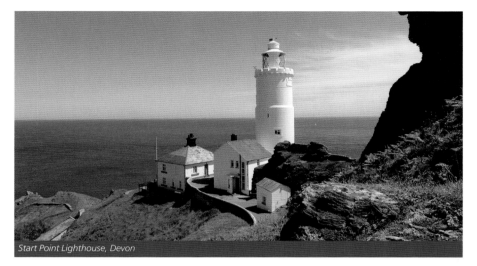

Start Point Lighthouse, Devon

STAY In Brighton or
Hove 0300 300 0088
visitbrighton.com

11 For the climb

Ardnamurchan
Lighthouse, Argyll
There are 152 steps and
two ladders to climb to reach
the top of Ardnamurchan
light tower but it's worth
the effort for the inspiring
views of the Inner and Outer
Hebrides when you get
there. Built in 1849 on the
most westerly point on the
British mainland – the only
one in the world in an
Egyptian style – it was
designed by Alan Stevenson,
uncle of Robert Louis; the
Stevensons being *the*

lighthouse family of the era.
It's made from pink granite
from the Isle of Mull and is
still fully operational. There's
a visitor centre in the old
engine room where you
can learn its history and
how the original foghorn
operated, plus a good café
in the restored stable block.
Open April to October.
Book ahead for a tour.
The Keeper's Cottage is
available for rent.
INFO 01972 510210
ardnamurchanlighthouse.
com
STAY In Ardnamurchan or
nearby Kilchoan 0845
2255121 visitscotland.com.
Keeper's Cottage 01972
510262 steading.co.uk

12 For the battlements

Start Point Lighthouse,
Devon
Standing 28 metres tall on
one of the most exposed
peninsulas on the Channel
coast, alongside the South
West Coast Path, the
castellated Start Point
Lighthouse dates from 1836.
It was automated in 1993
and is still fully operational.
If you arrange to stay in
one of the two cottages
alongside, bring earplugs
just in case it gets foggy:
the foghorn sounds every
60 seconds and can be
heard for miles around. See
website for opening times.
Tours take 45 minutes. There

Mull of Galloway Lighthouse, near Stranraer

14 For a dramatic crossing
South Stack Lighthouse, Anglesey

Perched on a small island known as South Stack Rock, the lighthouse is reached via 400 steps down the mainland cliffs and then across a metal-framed footbridge over the waves. Seabirds nest in the cliffs all the way down, so a pair of binoculars is a must for species-spotting along the way, especially in spring, and there are great views across the Irish Sea and the Welsh shore. Dramatic coastlines lead to dramatic events, none more so than during the 'storm of the century' in October 1859, when 200 vessels and 800 lives were lost around the area and South Stack keeper Jack Jones was one of the casualties. Open April to September. See website for opening times.
INFO South Stack Lighthouse 01248 724444 trinityhouse.co.uk
STAY In Anglesey 0845 074 0587 discoveranglesey.com

are great beaches nearby, such as Slapton Sands, Blackpool Sands and East Portlemouth.
INFO Start Point Lighthouse 01803 771802 trinityhouse.co.uk
STAY In Dartmouth or Salcombe 01803 834224 or 01548 843927 visitsouthdevon.co.uk. Lighthouse cottages 01386 701177 ruralretreats.co.uk

13 For gulls and grandeur
Mull of Galloway Lighthouse, near Stranraer

Peering from cliffs at the most southerly point on the Scottish mainland, this whitewashed tower was built in 1830 by Robert Stevenson, another of the talented Stevenson family and Robert Louis's grandfather. It is set within an RSPB reserve so there are plenty of opportunities for birdwatching. From the top you can see Antrim and the mountains of Mourne in Northern Ireland, the Isle of Man and the Lake District. Check website for opening times. The keeper's cottage is available to rent.
INFO Northern Lighthouse Board 0131 535 1314 nlb.org.uk
STAY Keepers Cottage 0131 243 9331 nts.org.uk, or elsewhere in Stranraer 01776 702595 visitscotland.com

Right: Llandudno Pier, Conwy

Weekends for art and music

The coast is a great place to tap into some culture. For centuries artists have been drawn to our coasts by the luminous quality of the light and by the tranquillity that can nurture a creative soul. The music scene thrives by the sea, too, so if you're looking for something to inspire and uplift you for a weekend, it could be the ideal destination. Browse around some artists' studios, watch a clifftop play, kick back at a summer music festival or sing along to some traditional shanties. All cultural life is here.

This page: Dylan Thomas Boathouse, Laugharne, Carmarthenshire

1 For artistic heritage

St Ives September Festival, Cornwall

There are always lots of good reasons to visit St Ives (artistic renown, great galleries, four beaches, stunning scenery, sub-tropical gardens…) but the September Festival of music and arts gives you an extra excuse, with musical performances, talks, poetry and workshops added to the mix. Music varies from jazz, blues and folk to classical concerts. Book tickets for performances in advance, to be on the safe side. While you're there, don't miss the beautifully atmospheric Barbara Hepworth Museum and Sculpture Garden, which features many of the sculptor's bronzes in the environment for which they were created; surely a highlight on anyone's cultural trail.

INFO stivesseptemberfestival. co.uk. Tate St Ives 01736 796226 tate.org.uk

STAY In St Ives or nearby Hayle 01736 796297 visitcornwall.com

Minack Theatre, Porthcurno, Cornwall

2 For joining in

Fishguard Folk Festival, Fishguard, Pembrokeshire

The Royal Oak pub in Fishguard's market square is at the heart of the town's annual Folk Festival, held over the late May Bank Holiday weekend. A mixture of concerts, dance displays, workshops, busking and meet-the-artist events make it a lively affair, teeming with jigging folksters. If you fancy yourself on the banjo or are a dab hand on the violin, you're encouraged to bring them with you, as impromptu jam sessions are a big part of the mix and anyone can join in. Most of the events are free and, of course, they're all accompanied by a fine range

of traditionally brewed ales to help loosen your tonsils for the sing-along. Check website for programme. INFO 01348 875183 pembrokeshire-folk-music. co.uk
STAY In Fishguard 01437 776636 visit-fishguard.org.uk, or walesdirectory.co.uk

3 For dramatic scenery
Minack Theatre, Porthcurno, Cornwall
You get more for your money when you see a production at the Minack

Theatre, near Penzance in Cornwall – the sight of a distant seal, perhaps, or a lone dolphin swimming by. It's this kind of added value that lures thousands of visitors to this clifftop, open-air attraction each summer. The 750-seat theatre in Porthcurno is a 20th century Roman-style amphitheatre, perched 200 feet above sea level with a stage hand-carved out of the cliff by its creator Rowena Cade, and fringed by classical pillars. The seating is mostly grassy terraces. Open all year for visitors; summer season of

productions runs from May to the end of September. INFO 01736810181 minack.com
STAY In Mousehole or nearby Penzance 01872 322900 visitcornwall.com

4 For being inquisitive
Artists Open Houses, Brighton, East Sussex
What could be a better way to shop for pressies (for yourself, of course, as well as for friends) than direct from the makers in their homes or studios and in a coastal setting? The main

Art on the Prom, Felixstowe, Suffolk

festival takes place over four weekends in May and there's a Christmas Open Houses event in late November/ early December. Alongside paintings and sculptures, you'll find ceramics, jewellery and textiles for sale. The May festival is the biggest event of its kind in Britain and there are usually more than 1,000 artists exhibiting their work at over 200 venues, across Brighton and Hove; the Christmas event is smaller but just as enticing. Most are arranged in trails, usually within walking distance of each other, so they are easy to link up. Entry is usually free. Check website for trails.

INFO aoh.org.uk
STAY In Brighton or Hove 0300 300 0088 visitbrighton.com

5 For musical escapism

Bestival, Robin Hill, Newport, Isle of Wight
Bestival is a three-day boutique music festival in September, the brainchild of DJ Rob da Bank as an offshoot of his Sunday Best record label and club nights. It has won 'Best Medium-sized Festival' at the UK Festival Awards for several years and it has also won an 'Outstanding' Greener Festival Award. The bands are a mixture of old and new – artists have included the likes of Kraftwerk, Florence and the Machine and The XX. Most people camp but there are yurt and tipi options or you can bring your own campervan or stay in a local B&B. Getting into a different persona for the weekend by dressing up is a big feature – the organisers describe it as 'a four-day wonderland of outlandish adventure and unparalleled escapism… fancy dress is the norm and tea and cake is always a good idea'. What could be better? It sells out early so book ahead.

INFO 020 7379 3133 bestival.net
STAY Camp at Bestival, IoW Tourist Information 01983 813813 islandbreaks.co.uk

6 For literary lovers

Laugharne Weekend Festival, Carmarthenshire
Laugharne was home to Wales's most famous poet and writer Dylan Thomas, who loved, drank and wrote here for the last four years of his life. It's an ancient town, sitting on the estuary of the River Taf – Thomas described it as the town where he 'got off the bus and never got on again'. At the annual literary festival, held in April, A-list musicians and writers flock to perform in small halls and pub back rooms around town and it's the kind of event Thomas might have enjoyed himself – intimate, funny and a little chaotic. Book in advance to avoid disappointment, especially for accommodation. Other attractions in the town include the ruin of Laugharne Castle, perched on the river's edge – evocative enough to bring out the poet in anyone, and Pendine's seven-mile stretch of sand, where attempts at the land speed record were made in the 1920s.

INFO thelaugharneweekend. com
STAY At Hurst House 01994 427417 hurst-house.co.uk, or elsewhere in Laugharne or nearby St Clears 01267 231557 discovercarmarthenshire.com

Right: Laugharne Weekend Festival is a must for keen readers

7 For beachside buys

Art on the Prom, Felixstowe, Suffolk

Seaside-themed art events are always enjoyable to browse through but this fair goes one better by taking place on the seafront promenade among the beach huts of this Edwardian resort. Art on the Prom has been running for several years and features 70 or 80 artists of all abilities – both hobby and professional – who display and sell their work in the fresh sea air. If the works on show bring a sudden rush of creativity to your head and you are inspired to put paint to paper yourself, you can join one of the Art in the Gardens 'have-a-go' workshops. Led by artists, you'll be encouraged to paint or tie-dye, make a plaster cast or weave some willow. In between times, watch out for stilt walkers, jugglers, magicians and other street entertainers along the prom. It's an all-day event and is usually held on a Sunday in late August/early September. Check website for date and times.

INFO 01394 671033 artontheprom.org

STAY In Felixstowe or nearby Aldeburgh 01394 276770 and 01728 453637 suffolkcoastal.gov.uk

8 For a jaunty sing-along

Falmouth International Sea Shanty Festival, Falmouth, Cornwall

Sea shanties are having a bit of a moment and the Falmouth International Sea

Bestival, Robin Hill, Newport, Isle of Wight

Shanty Festival is the place to hear the best of the bunch. The rousing call and response style, originally developed as rhythms to help sailors perform their rope-hauling, anchor-raising and sail-trimming duties at sea, can't fail to get you tapping your foot and wanting to join in the chorus. Performers come from all over the south-west and abroad, sporting names such as Falmouth Shout, Stamp & Go, Shake-a-Leg and Fisherman's Friends (who were signed to a major record label last year).
INFO 01326 373 603
falmouthshout.com
STAY In Falmouth or nearby Penryn 01326 312300
discoverfalmouth.co.uk

9 For chamber music

East Neuk Festival,
Crail, Fife

This quirky annual festival, held in July, has carved out its own distinctive niche in the British summer festival circuit by offering world-class chamber music performed in unusual venues along East Neuk's coastline, from tiny churches in picturesque fishing villages to stately Holy Trinity Church in St Andrews. All are wonderfully atmospheric, adding greatly to the ambience of the event. Featured composers include Brahms, Britten, Beethoven, Mozart and Vaughan Williams among many more. And when you've had your fill of music you can retire to any one of East Neuk's numerous good beaches, including the golden sands of Elie.
INFO 0131 669 1750
eastneukfestival.com
STAY In Crail or nearby Anstruther 01333 450869 (Crail Tourist Information), or visitfife.com

East Neuk Festival, Crail, Fife

Artist Jane Carbrera at work in south Devon

10 For funky dancing

Caister Soul Weekender, Great Yarmouth, Norfolk

The Caister Soul Weekender (named after the original location at Caister on Sea) is the UK's largest and longest-running soul music event and has been pulling in the punters since the 1970s. Its mix of friendly, feelgood frolics is aimed at anyone who loves a dance, a drink and a lot of get-down-on-it funky soul. It's brash, bright and care-free – this is the most fun you can have dancing for three days with the UK's top soul DJs. There are several venues, playing soul and funk from the past four decades, barbecue parties and a fancy dress night with a different theme every time. Party-goers – mostly fun-loving 40-year-olds – stay either on site at the Vauxhall Pleasure Gardens holiday camp or in local hotels or campsites. It's held twice a year, in May and October.

INFO 0844 585 1000
weekenders.co.uk
STAY In Great Yarmouth
01493 846345
great-yarmouth.co.uk

11 For a tribute to Elvis

Elvis Festival, Porthcawl, Glamorgan

For more Elvises than you can shake a hip at, get along to the annual Elvis Festival in the seaside town of Porthcawl which the organisers claim is 'the largest festival of its kind in the world'. Each September, on Glamorgan's Heritage Coast, Elvis Tribute Artists and thousands of fans from around the world gather to sing, compete and pay homage to their hero in a surreal three-day extravaganza, *The Elvies*. There is an Elvis for everyone: GI Elvis, Black Leather Elvis, Early Rocker Elvis… but the most popular by far is Las Vegas Elvis, complete with rhinestones and sideburns. The performance schedules are tighter than a sequinned catsuit, so artistes speed from Heartbreak Hotel (real name The Brentwood) to the stage, singing their hearts out to appreciative audiences. Shows take place in the Grand Pavilion, Porthcawl's Art Deco theatre perched on the seafront, and are described as the full-blown 'Elvis in Vegas' floor show experience, followed by an Elvis disco party. This is paradise, Porthcawl style!

INFO elvies.co.uk
STAY The Brentwood Hotel 01656 782725 thebrentwoodhotel.co.uk, or elsewhere in Porthcawl or nearby Barry 01656 786639 bridgend.gov.uk

12 For behind the scenes

Devon Open Studios, various locations, Devon
Held annually in September, Devon Open Studios is one of the highlights of Devon's cultural calendar, offering you the chance to visit artists in their homes and studios in locations throughout the county. Studios range from medieval barns and glassblowing workshops to sleek city centre galleries, and more than 250 artists take part over about 16 days in all, taking in three weekends. The variety of work is far-ranging and includes painting, drawing, printmaking, sculpture, ceramics, photography, textiles, jewellery, collage, works in glass, metal, wood and paper, furniture making and more. Entry to all studios is free and many artists give demonstrations or talks or will give you the chance to have a go yourself. You might be offered a cream tea here and there, too. Events are held in seven different areas – see the event guide for details.
INFO 07768 164560 devonartistnetwork.co.uk
STAY visitdevon.co.uk, or Helpful Holidays (self-catering cottages) 01647 433593 helpfulholidays.com

Elvis Festival, Porthcawl, Glamorgan

Pebbles

We have all picked a pebble off the beach and marvelled at it. But where do they come from and what kind of rock is each one? How old are they? After being weathered for millennia,

Granite

IDENTIFYING FEATURES Overall, it has a greyish appearance, but a closer look reveals components of shiny quartz, white felspar and black mica.
WHERE TO FIND South-west England, Cumbria and north-east Scotland.
A CURIOUS THING Often used in construction, because it is so hard and durable. Fishermen's cottages on the Cornish coast are usually made from granite.

Flint

IDENTIFYING FEATURES This hard stone often has sharp, twisted edges. It is grey/brown in colour, though sometimes coated in pale chalky stone.
WHERE TO FIND Widespread around the UK – plentiful in south Devon and Sussex.
A CURIOUS THING Flint can produce a spark if struck hard.

Quartz

IDENTIFYING FEATURES Quartz pebbles are pale, almost transparent, and are often small and irregular in shape. Colours can vary from clear and cloudy white through to pink, brown and mauve shades.
WHERE TO FIND On most pebble or gravel beaches.
A CURIOUS THING Quartz digital watches are famously precise, based on quartz's electric potential.

washed back and forth by the tide, pebbles can look dirty white or grey at first. You may have to scrape back the surface to reveal the identity of the rock underneath but the effort is worthwhile to give you an insight into the geology of the area you are in. If you want to take pebbles from a beach, check local bylaws first to see if you are able to do so.

Jet

IDENTIFYING FEATURES A black, lightweight, coal-like stone, popular for ornaments. Will burn with a greenish flame.

WHERE TO FIND The Yorkshire coast is famous for its jet – especially Whitby.

A CURIOUS THING After the death of her beloved Prince Albert, Queen Victoria popularised wearing jet as mourning jewellery.

Schist

IDENTIFYING FEATURES A finely grained, dark- or light-grey, striped rock that can be broken easily.

WHERE TO FIND On the shores of Wales or Cornwall.

A CURIOUS THING Most schists have been derived from clays and muds. Schist can be found all around the world and is popular with collectors.

Serpentine

IDENTIFYING FEATURES Usually green, but sometimes red, this pebble is very attractive, with a soft, waxy feel. Before it is washed smooth by the sea, serpentine is scaly like snakeskin.

WHERE TO FIND On the Lizard Peninsula in Cornwall.

A CURIOUS THING Serpentine is easily worked into lamp holders, paperweights and bowls so makes a popular souvenir from craft shops.

Weekends for running and cycling

Swap the airless gym and the local park and traffic-clogged roads for some healthy sea air. Beach running might be harder than the treadmill, but you get twice the benefit and the views beat anything you could see on the gym wall. Cycling along a clifftop or converted railway line is a terrific way to take in sweeping ocean views and spot wildlife along the way. Pack your trainers and grab the cycle clips – we have found cycle networks and places to run that will renew your enthusiasm for getting active and energise your spirit.

This page: Checking the map on the coastal path

NCN numbers refer to National Cycle Network routes, which run all over Great Britain. These can be accessed on the Sustrans website – sustrans.org.uk – and downloaded as mapped guides.

1 For dramatic scenery

Cullen to Garmouth, Moray (NCN 1; 14 miles)

This quiet, well-signed cycle route offers spectacular views from craggy cliffs over the Moray Firth, where you might be lucky enough to spot harbour porpoises and bottlenose dolphins. The latter often leap clear out of the water. Travel over the old railway viaduct in Cullen, before following the path to the rock arch of Bow Fiddle Rock and the village of Portknockie. Next is Findochty (pronounced 'Finnechty') with its pretty cottages and boat-filled harbour, followed by the village of Port Gordon and then Garmouth. Follow the railway path east across the Speyside Viaduct to the Whale and Dolphin Conservation Society (WDCS) Wildlife Centre at Spey Bay, where you can spot bottlenose dolphins with the binoculars and telescopes provided, listen live to their underwater noises and make a pit stop at the café.

INFO Sustrans 0845 113 00 65 sustrans.org.uk. Moray Firth Wildlife Centre 01343 820339 wdcs.org.uk

STAY In or around Cullen 0845 2255121 visitscotland.com

2 For views from the saddle

King's Lynn to Cromer, Norfolk (Regional Route 30; 60 miles)

This newly created cycleway on the west Norfolk coastline winds past a mixture of rolling sand dunes, reed beds and crystal-clear horizons. You'll pass the medieval ruins at Castle Rising with its stone keep and massive earthworks. Carry on via the Queen's Norfolk residence at Sandringham and arrive at Ringstead – the perfect place

Bottlenose dolphin, Moray Firth

to stop for a meal and an overnight stay at The Gin Trap Inn, a 17th century coaching inn. The next day, pass country churches and Holkham Park on the way to Cromer.

INFO Sustrans 0845 113 00 65 sustrans.org.uk. Norfolk Coast Area of Outstanding Natural Beauty norfolkcoastaonb.org.uk STAY The Gin Trap Inn 01485 525264 gintrapinn.co.uk. Cromer Tourist Information 0871 200 3071 visitnorthnorfolk.com

3 For good old-fashioned charm
Colwyn Bay to Prestatyn, Conwy and Denbighshire (NCN 5; 19 miles)
With the fresh salty breeze on your face, cycle down the wide sea promenade beside the three-mile stretch of Colwyn Bay's sand, past award-winning beaches and Gwrych Castle in the hills between Llanddulas and Abergele. Local Colwyn Bay cyclists stop off at the Pantri Bach café at Abergele for a cuppa and an 'Onslow', more commonly known as a bacon butty. Suitably refuelled, you can press on

to Rhyl and Prestatyn, two of the most atmospheric seaside towns in Wales. If you cycle the route in the opposite direction, carry on up to Rhos-on-Sea to visit the tiny 16th century chapel of St Trillo, thought to be the smallest church in Britain.
INFO Sustrans 0845 113 00 65 sustrans.org.uk, or cyclingnorthwales.co.uk STAY In Colwyn Bay or Prestatyn 01492 531731 nwt.co.uk

4 For active families
Whitby to Scarborough, North Yorkshire (NCN 1; 18 miles)
Gather the clan for this fun off-road coastal path, which is part of the Moor to Sea cycle route, largely following the old railway track bed.

From Whitby's railway path, cycle along open moorland and through to Ravenscar where you can stop off at the Ravenscar Coastal Centre to discover more about the local landscape. The beach at Hayburn Wyke is another highlight and there are places to eat and drink in Cloughton and Hayburn Wyke in case anyone's energy is flagging. Once at Scarborough, check out Peasholm Park at North Bay where you can get ice-creams and explore round the lake.
INFO Sustrans 0845 113 00 65 sustrans.org.uk. Also moortoseacycle.net. National Trust Peakside 01723 870423 nationaltrust.org.uk STAY Yorkshire Coast Tourist

Whitby to Scarborough, North Yorkshire

Information 01723 383636
discoveryorkshirecoast.com

5 For easy riders

Pembrey to Bynea,
Carmarthenshire (NCN 4;
14 miles)

The Millennium Coastal
Park is a ten-mile stretch of
coastline on the Burry Estuary,
perfect for young or nervous
cyclists, as you can glide
along on a smooth coastal
cycleway. It is purpose built
and traffic free, following the
coast all the way along. The
whole area used to be
industrial wasteland and it
was reclaimed for the new
millennium to be transformed
into a tranquil green corridor.
The surface is a mixture of
tarmac and gravel paths so it
makes easy riding. Highlights
include superb views of the
Gower Peninsula, the
Discovery Centre overlooking
Llanelli beach and the new
marina at Burry Port.
INFO Sustrans 0845
113 00 65 sustrans.org.uk.
Millennium Coastal Park
carmarthenshire.gov.uk.
Discovery Centre
01554 777744
STAY In Pembrey or
Penclacwydd 01267 231557
discovercarmarthenshire.com

6 For sightseeing

Giant's Causeway to
Benone, County Antrim
(NCN 93; 22 miles)

This cycle route along the
North Atlantic coast has a
smorgasbord of attractions.
It takes you along the north
coast of County Antrim,
following National Cycle
Network 93 between the
Giant's Causeway in the
east and Benone in the west,
passing through Portrush,
Portstewart and Castlerock.
You can see the full route
on the Cycle Northern
Ireland website and
download a map. Don't
miss out on a stop-off at
the Bushmills Distillery in –
you guessed it – Bushmills,
where you can quaff a
dram of Irish whiskey.
INFO Cycle Northern Ireland
028 9030 3930 cycleni.com
STAY In Castlerock or
Portrush 028 7082 3333
discovernorthernireland.com

7 For a challenge

The Pembrokeshire Half
Marathon, Dale,
Pembrokeshire

The route for this testing
half-marathon (annually,
on the last Sunday in
September) starts and
finishes in the unspoilt
village of Dale in the heart
of the Pembrokeshire Coast
National Park. Before long,
you'll be sweating your way
over St Ann's Head, enjoying
views across to Milford
Haven, before returning
inland. The coast is never
far away, and there's an
abundance of wildlife along
the way; you'll soon see
Skomer Island, a vital
breeding ground for the
Manx shearwater. For those
who'd prefer a gentler
challenge, there is a 10km
run on the same day. You
need to enter for both
events in advance. Check
Pembrokeshire Triathlon
Club website for dates.
INFO Pembrokeshire Triathlon
Club 07975 925365 (Milford
Haven Tourist Information)
pembrokeshire-tri.org.uk
STAY In Dale 01437 771818
visitpembrokeshire.com

8 For maritime history

Plymouth Hoe, Devon

It may be apocryphal, but
who can resist the thought
of Sir Francis Drake playing a
game of bowls on Plymouth

*Right: Hayburn Wyke from
Cleveland Way, North Yorkshire*

Hoe, before sailing to do battle with the Spanish Armada? Run along the Hoe today and you'll encounter Smeaton's Tower, with its views of Plymouth Sound, and the Royal Citadel, which, for more than 100 years after its construction in the late 17th century, was England's most important defensive outpost. Beneath the Hoe is the Tinside Pool, an Art Deco lido with fantastic views – just the spot, from May to September, to cool off after running this stretch of the coastline. Tower and Citadel are open May to September for tours. Call in to the Tourist Information Centre for a free map of the Hoe, Barbican and city centre. INFO Plymouth Tourist Information 01752 306330 plymouth.gov.uk STAY In Plymouth or nearby Looe 01752 306330 visitplymouth.co.uk

9 For the intrepid

The Viking Coastal Trail, Kent

This popular peninsula route, at 27 miles, takes in the historic seaside towns of Broadstairs and Margate, and offers runners and cyclists miles of clear seashore track along England's most easterly coastal point. It encompasses 15 sandy bays, nature reserves and the panoramic Joss Bay, a popular surfing beach. Better still, you can tackle the Viking Trail in bite-sized chunks, with enticing names like Smugglers' Haunts, Beaches and Bays and Six Churches. The Historic Broadstairs route is three and a quarter

The Great North Run, Tyne & Wear

miles, while the path of St Augustine, taking in Minster Abbey, is four and a half miles.
INFO 0870 264 6111 visitthanet.co.uk/Viking
STAY In Margate, Broadstairs or villages en route 01843 577577 visitthanet.co.uk

10 For running pedigree

The Great North Run, Tyne & Wear

If you want to enter the world's most popular half-marathon, which runs annually in September, put your name down for the Great North Run. Ten thousand runners took part in the first one in 1981, now it attracts more than 50,000 entrants and comprises a gruelling circuit starting in Newcastle before crossing the famous Tyne Bridge. Competitors then run through Gateshead and South Tyneside before finishing on the dramatic South Shields coast.
INFO Great Run Series greatrun.org
STAY In South Shields 0191 454 6612 visitsouthtyneside.co.uk

11 For families

Orcombe Point to Exmouth Marina, Devon

Exmouth has two miles of golden sand, and families who love a gentle run should head along the promenade from Orcombe Point to the Marina. Orcombe Point marks the western end of the World Heritage Coast, (which runs much further along, to Old Harry Rocks in Dorset). This first leg is flat all the way and, if you need refreshments, there are cafés and ice-cream kiosks. The Grove – a family- and dog-friendly pub – is perfect for a post-run lunch. If it's warm enough you can sit outside in the grassy garden overlooking the sea.
INFO Exmouth Tourist Information 01395 222299 exmouth-guide.co.uk, or jurassiccoast.com.
The Grove 01395 272101 groveexmouth.com
STAY Exmouth Tourist Information 01395 222299 exmouth-guide.co.uk

12 For splendid isolation

Holkham Beach, Norfolk

The feeling of solitude you get on these endless sands,

and in the surrounding pinewoods, makes for a truly uplifting seaside experience. No wonder Holkham Beach was voted Best Beach in the coast Awards 2010. The three-and-three-quarter-mile stretch of Holkham sands and the dunes, known locally as the Holkham Meals, really do seem to go on for ever. In summer, the beach – immortalised by Gwyneth Paltrow in the closing scenes of *Shakespeare in Love* – is popular with families and tourists. Even so, it's expansive enough for you to enjoy the delicious loneliness of the long-distance runner. Part of a National Nature Reserve managed by Natural England, Holkham and its rolling dunes, saltflats and pine woods are inhabited by a wide variety of birds and wildlife. See the Holkham website for suggested routes.
INFO Holkham Estate 01328 710227 holkham.co.uk.
Natural England 0845 600 3078 naturalengland.org.uk
STAY In Holkham or Wells-Next-the-Sea 01328 710885 visitnorthnorfolk.com

Weekends
for swimming

The advent of the wetsuit has meant there is no excuse for not enjoying British seas. Sea swimming is exhilarating and it also has numerous benefits for your mind, body and spirit. We have found some magical places to swim and snorkel – sandy coves that are hard to reach on foot, secluded bays for bodysurfing in the breakers, rocky pools and west-facing beaches for a sunset dip. Go for an invigorating swim in the ocean and you'll return from your weekend thoroughly revived and springing with energy.

This page: The exhilaration of the surf, Brighton, East Sussex

Be beach safe

On lifeguard-patrolled beaches, look out for red-and-yellow flags and swim between them; red flags mean Danger, do not swim. On beaches without lifeguards, you'll obviously need to take extra precautions and know your own limitations. Always swim with someone, never alone; check local tides, currents and weather conditions, and if in doubt, don't go out. For useful sea swimming advice see wildswimming.co.uk and safewatersports.co.uk.

1 For sandy coves

Church Bay, Anglesey

Ancient Anglesey, a land of burial cairns and Neolithic sites, contains some of the finest sand coves on the North Wales coast, as well as some of its most dramatic coastal features, from caves and arches to volcanic lava flows. For a real treat, swim from Church Bay, also known as Porth Swtan, a beautiful white sand cove, between Carmel Head and Holy Island on the north-west of Anglesey, edged by rockpools and backed by steep cliffs. Reached by a footpath from the village, it gets its name from the nearby St Rhyddlad's Church, Llanrhyddlad, visible from the bay.

INFO 01248 713177 visitanglesey.co.uk

STAY In Holyhead or nearby Treaddur Bay 01248 713177 visitanglesey.co.uk

2 For sporty types

The Brighton Pier to Pier Swim, East Sussex

A small band of plucky seabathers take to the water almost every day of the year in Brighton so you'll always have someone to swim with

The Brighton Pier to Pier Swim, East Sussex

The Blue Lagoon, Abereiddy, Pembrokeshire

here. The annual Brighton Pier to Pier Swim is held every summer (see website for date) and hundreds of swimming club members of all abilities dive into the surf for the glory of winning a coveted trophy. Just about a mile long, the course runs between the now derelict West Pier and Brighton (Palace) Pier. Hire a deckchair and watch the myriad brightly coloured, numbered swimming caps bobbing along from the safety of the shore or take a swim nearby. INFO Brighton Swimming Club brightonsc.co.uk STAY In Brighton 0300 300 0088 visitbrighton.com

3 For liberated swimmers
Forty Foot, Sandycove, Dublin
The Forty Foot is a deep seawater inlet where people have come to swim for at least 250 years. Set amid the rugged rock-strewn coast in Sandycove, eight

miles from Dublin and just south of Dun Laoghaire, it was once preserved as gentlemen only but thanks to the women's lib movement it is now open to all. Past swimmers include James Joyce, hence the James Joyce Tower, a Martello tower built in 1804 as one of a series commissioned by William Pitt to withstand an invasion by Napoleon. The spirit of Ireland's greatest writer infuses not just his tower but also the seawater bathing area. Glide through the water and plot your novel. See Forty Foot's website for tide details and location. INFO fortyfoot.org STAY In Sandycove, Dun Laoghaire or Dublin, Tourism Ireland 08000 397000 discoverireland.com

4 For lagoon bathing
The Blue Lagoon, Abereiddy, Pembrokeshire
This beach, with its 470-million-year-old rock forms, has pebbles and sand made from pounded grey slate and at one end is the spectacular Blue Lagoon, a flooded former slate quarry with

beautiful deep-blue water. Although largely cut off from the ebb and flow of the sea, the lagoon, regarded as an important geological feature, does have a tidal channel to the sea, so bathers need to be careful. There are no lifeguards here, and a west-facing direction means that a large swell can create turbulence. Nevertheless, if you are a confident swimmer, this is definitely one to try.

INFO Oriel y Parc Information Centre 01437 720392 orielyparc.co.uk
STAY In Abereiddy or St David's 01437 776636 visitpembrokeshire.com

5 For pure surf appeal

Bodysurfing, Woolacombe, Devon

Long before anyone thought of making a surfboard, people were swimming out through breakers and bodysurfing back to shore. All you really need is a swimming costume and a bit of nerve, although specialised swimfins to help you paddle faster are a great advantage. The best bodysurfers compete in the Wold Bodysurfing Championships in Hawaii, but it's too far for a weekend, so stay closer to home on the three-mile-long sandy beach of Woolacombe in north Devon. It is a great place for this purest form of surfing – it was once voted Britain's best resort for family fun and it retains an easy-going charm, with lifeguards on patrol throughout the summer.

INFO 01271 870 553 woolacombetourism.co.uk
STAY In Woolacombe or nearby Croyde 01271 870553 woolacombetourism.co.uk, or visitdevon.co.uk

6 For distant sand dunes

Tyrella, County Down

A small enclosed dune complex within Dundrum Bay, Tyrella is a wide, flat, sandy beach, a mile and a half long and backed by 25 hectares of mature dunes. This is a conservation area so it's a great place to walk and swim, having been awarded the prestigious Seaside Award annually since 1997. As with many beaches in Northern Ireland, it's cleaner than ever, thanks to a £240 million investment in sewage-treatment infrastructure. As well as safe swimming, the beach offers a car-free zone, off-beach parking and a tourist information centre nearby.

INFO Tyrella Tourist Information 028 4482 8333 delamontcountrypark.com
STAY In Tyrella or Downpatrick 028 4461 2233 discovernorthernireland.com

7 For family fun

Praa Sands, Cornwall

Praa Sands, a few miles from St Michael's Mount in west Cornwall, is an unpretentious English beach, where buckets and spades are more important than looking cool. With over a mile of south-facing golden sands to play on, it's also a great place to swim with children, especially at low tide in the summer. There are rockpools galore so there's plenty of exploring to be done. Keep your eyes peeled and you are likely to see feeding terns, auks and gannets – and if you are fortunate, you might glimpse some passing dolphins or porpoises. From spring through to

Right: Forty Foot, Sandycove, Dublin

Budleigh Salterton, Devon

Everything here is elegant, restrained and, yes, genteel. That goes for the swimming too. Positioned in the middle of a beautiful bay on the western side of the River Otter estuary, the shelving pebble beach offers bathing in clear, blue water. The name Salterton is derived from the days when the town's main industry was salt panning. It is just off the South West Coast Path so it's a popular stopping-off point for long-distance walkers and the fish and chips at the Premier Café are a real treat. INFO 01395 445275 budleighsalterton.org STAY In Budleigh Salterton or Topsham 01395 445275 visitbudleigh.com, or visitdevon.co.uk

9 For solitude
Isle of Staffa, Outer Hebrides

Staffa is a volcanic isle, one of the smallest in the southern Hebrides, best known for its many caves including the fabled Fingal's Cave. A natural sound chamber, the acoustics of this very special spot inspired Mendelssohn to compose his *Hebrides Overture*. Hexagonal basalt

autumn there are also many butterflies and moths attracted by the abundant wild flowers of the area. INFO Penzance Tourist Information 01736 362207 visitcornwall.com, or praasands.info STAY In Praa Sands or nearby Porthleven 01872 322900 visitcornwall.com

8 For a gentle dip
Budleigh Salterton, Devon

In an Area of Outstanding Natural Beauty on the east coast of Devon, Budleigh Salterton is a gem of a town.

columns rise like organ pipes to its ceiling and plunge down to the depths. It is possible to walk to the cave overland, where a row of fractured columns form a walkway just above high-water level. Boats operate April to October from Mull and Iona or you can get a tour deal from the mainland at Oban. Staffa is uninhabited, so find a base on Mull or Iona.

INFO 08707 200 630 southernhebrides.com

STAY 0845 2255121 visitscotland.com, or holidaymull.co.uk

10 For wild swimming

Rushy Bay, Bryher, Isles of Scilly

Follow in the slipstream of the book that started the craze: in this shallow sandy bay on the sheltered south-eastern side of the island, writer Roger Deakin began *Waterlog*, his swimmer's journey through Britain. 'It was high tide and about thirty yards off the shore I looked down at a pair of stone walls... and a circle of stones that must once have been a sheep pen.' The submerged field patterns testify to a time when the islands of Bryher, Samson and Tresco were linked and – before the flood caused by the melting of the polar ice caps 4,000 years ago – formed part of the island of Ennor. Bryher is the smallest of the inhabited islands and you can walk around it on the coastal paths in a couple of hours.

INFO 01720 424031 simplyscilly.co.uk

STAY On Bryher or Tresco 01720 424031 simplyscilly.co.uk

Praa Sands, Cornwall

11 For warm waters
West Wittering, West
Sussex

Consistently recommended for its water quality, West Wittering has a vast sandy beach for children to play on when the tide is out. On an incoming tide the water heats up over the warm sand, creating a water temperature that can be more akin to the Caribbean in the summer months. The sea is popular with all sorts of users, from swimmers to kite- and windsurfers, so it can get busy at times. To refuel after your dip there's the Beach Café, with a coffee shop and takeaway. INFO West Wittering Beach 01243 514143 westwitteringbeach.co.uk STAY In West Wittering 01243 775 888 visitchichester.org, or nearby Bognor Regis 01243 823140 sussexbythesea.com

12 For a breezy dip
Rhosneigr, Anglesey

There are miles of uncrowded sand at Rhosneigr so you'll have plenty of room to spread out before you go in for your dip. Prevailing westerly winds also make this a Mecca for kite surfers so you should see plenty of action. It is a magnificent open bay, with outcrops of rock effectively breaking up the beach into sheltered coves, where you can rest out of the wind. Situated on the west coast of Anglesey, you'll have sweeping views of the Snowdonia mountains and Llyn Peninsula. Once a famous Edwardian holiday

Fingal's Cave, Isle of Staffa, Outer Hebrides

retreat, Rhosneigr still attracts families.
INFO 01248 713177 visitanglesey.co.uk
STAY In Rhosneigr or nearby Aberffraw 01248 713177 visitanglesey.co.uk

13 For great views

Bouley Bay, Jersey

Steep, heather-clad cliffs provide the dramatic backdrop for the north coast of Jersey, which makes it a popular venue for summer hill-climb races organised by the quaintly named Jersey Motor Cycle and Light Car Club. Drop down to Bouley Bay and you find a small harbour and a far-reaching beach of pebble and rock that has become the unofficial home of scuba diving on the island, largely due to the clear, deep water. There's good swimming to be had, although as the water is deep you need to be a strong swimmer. The views here are spectacular; on a clear day you can see the French coast. The high cliffs backing the beach mean that the bay loses the sun in the afternoon so maybe that's the time to retreat to the Beach Café

Taking to the sea in late afternoon

or the Black Dog Bar for a reviving drink.

INFO 01534 448877 jersey.com

STAY In Bouley Bay or elsewhere on the island 01534 448888 jersey.com

14 For watching wildlife

Gairloch, Redpoint North, Highlands

This sand and pebble beach is set against the backdrop of the mountains of Skye, characterised by red-hued sand and sheltered from the Highland winds by grassy dunes. Swimmers are also rewarded with a huge variety of marine life including spiralling gannets, sea eagles, otters and the occasional porpoise.

INFO Ullapool Tourist Information 01854 612486 visitscotland.com

STAY In Gairloch or nearby villages in Wester Ross 0845 2255121 visitscotland.com

15 For a shot at the Channel

Shakespeare Beach, Dover, Kent

Just to the west of Dover, Shakespeare Beach is a long, secluded shingle beach with deep rockpools and wave-cut platforms, backed by monumental white cliffs. One of its main claims to fame is that it is a noted jumping-off point for Channel swimmers because the 18.2 nautical miles (approximately 21 land miles) to Cap Gris Nez is the shortest distance between England and France. Even if you're not planning to go all the way, it seems a great place to have a symbolic dip and pay tribute to those brave souls who do.

INFO Dover Tourist Information 01304 205108 whitecliffscountry.org.uk

STAY In Dover or nearby Walmer or Deal 01304 205108 whitecliffscountry.org.uk

16 For skinny dipping

Fishing Cove, Godrevy Point, Cornwall

Cast off your inhibitions along with your clothes and enjoy a few hours in the fresh air with little to worry about but the application of some suncream. This beautiful little cove on the north Cornish coast, between Portreath and Hayle is popular with naturists for the great swimming and, goosebumps aside, it is easy to understand the appeal. Popular with locals and tourists alike, it is a steep climb down to the sandy beach, which is backed by cliffs giving plenty of shade. There are great views and one visitor has described it as 'tranquil and peaceful with a desert island feel'. Park at the National Trust car park and head west to take the path down. Swimmers say currents can make it challenging if it's windy, but otherwise it's a secret cove well worth seeking out.

INFO Naturist UK Fact File nuff.org.uk

STAY In Hayle or St Ives 01736 796297 visitcornwall.com

Right: Preparing for the elements, Brighton, East Sussex

Weekends for surfing

Surfing has never been so popular, so don't let your age or ability put you off taking out a board. There are surf schools popping up all around the coast, with patient and inspiring teachers ready to show you how it's done. Just a few short lessons will have you standing up and gliding shorewards – which, if you have never tried it before, can seem like nothing short of a miracle. If you are already a seasoned surfer and want to hone your skills, check out some of these exciting new places to polish your curves.

This page: Getting to grips with a surfboard at Croyde Bay, Devon

Fistral Beach, Newquay, Cornwall

1 For surfing history

Fistral Beach, Newquay, Cornwall

The epicentre of UK surfing, Fistral is the home of the British Surfing Association and hosts the Relentless Boardmasters, Britain's biggest surfing event, every August. No wonder, because when the conditions are right, Fistral's wide, sandy beach serves up some of the best waves the UK has to offer. But, as befits the town in which British surfing first took root in the early 1960s, there are plenty of surf schools catering for beginners. One of the best is provided by the English Surfing Federation (ESF), a short walk from Fistral at Carnmarth Hotel. Lessons last for two hours; use of equipment is included. INFO ESF Surf School 01637 879571 englishsurfschool.com STAY In Newquay or nearby Perranporth 01872 322900 visitcornwall.com

2 For a chilled-out vibe

Sennen Cove, Cornwall

An exquisite bay in the far west of Cornwall, Sennen Cove has a chilled-out vibe that dates back to the early 1970s, when the area was the home of Skewjack, Britain's one and only surf village. There are two local surf schools – Sennen Surfing Centre, underneath the award-winning Beach restaurant, and Smart Surf, on the esplanade. Both are excellent but to rub shoulders with an elite athlete, contact Smart Surf, one of whose instructors, Sam, is both a pro surfer and a pro boxer. INFO Sennen Surfing Centre 01736 871227 sennensurfingcentre.com and Smart Surf 01736 871817 smartsurf.co.uk. Beach Restaurant 01736 871191 thebeachrestaurant.com STAY In Sennen Cove or nearby St Just 01872 322900 visitcornwall.com

3 For all mod cons

Watergate Bay, Cornwall

With its chic and relaxed Hotel & Extreme Academy, Watergate Bay was set up to be 'a ski resort on the beach'. It offers just about every water sport imaginable and even has a celebrity chef restaurant on its doorstep with the Jamie Oliver inspired Fifteen Cornwall. Just a few miles from Newquay airport,

The Hotel & Extreme Academy is also handy for those who want to fly rather than drive to the surf. A half-day lesson can be booked through the Extreme Academy and private lessons can also be arranged.
INFO Extreme Academy 01637 860840 watergatebay.co.uk. Fifteen Cornwall 01637 861000 fifteencornwall.co.uk
STAY The Hotel 01637 860543 watergatebay.co.uk, or in nearby Newquay 01872 322900 visitcornwall.com

4 For northern soul
Saltburn-by-the-Sea, Redcar & Cleveland
The elegant Victorian town of Saltburn is a gem, with a wide, sandy beach and an immense headland jutting out into the North Sea. Saltburn is also one of the original hotbeds of the north-east surf scene, thanks to good beginner waves either side of the pier. Saltburn Surf School, above the beach, can provide everything from lessons, hire and advice, while the Surf Shop can kit you out with a new board or wetsuit.
INFO Saltburn Surf 07961 714993 saltburnsurf.co.uk. Surf Shop 01287 625321
STAY In Saltburn or nearby Redcar 01287 622422 visitteesvalley.co.uk

5 For mellow longboarding
Saunton Sands, Braunton, Devon
A big tide range and gently sloping beach make Saunton's three miles of sand a must for anyone surfing a

A helping hand from Sennen Surfing Centre, Sennen Cove, Cornwall

longboard. These boards have the planing ability to make the most of the classic slow waves here. If you're not in the water yourself, watch the surfers' long sweeping rides from the cliff road above the bay and, if you're inspired to have a go, you'll find the shallows ideal for beginners. Surfing equipment can be hired on the beach or in Braunton village. The beach is home to the award-winning Saunton Sands Surf Life Saving Club, whose members are trained in life saving skills.

INFO Surf Life Saving Club sauntonirb.co.uk
STAY In Saunton Sands or nearby Braunton 01271 816400 brauntontic.co.uk, or 01752 306330 visitdevon.co.uk

6 For a vibrant surf scene

Belhaven Bay, East Lothian
The north coast of Scotland boasts one of the world's best waves in the reef break at Thurso East, but it's strictly for experts only. Further south, close to Edinburgh, there is a vibrant surf scene and an excellent place to

Saltburn-by-the-Sea, Redcar & Cleveland

learn in the form of the Coast to Coast Surf School. Located at Belhaven Bay, near Dunbar, instructors are all British Surfing Association qualified and offer lessons from March to November. They'll also take you on surf tours to some quality waves.

INFO Coast to Coast Surf School 07971 990361 c2csurfschool.com
STAY In Dunbar or North Berwick 01368 863353 and 01620 892197 visiteastlothian.org or visitscotland.com

7 For big waves and vistas

The Gower Peninsula, near Swansea
In the first designated Area of Outstanding Natural Beauty in the UK, numerous beaches offer quality year-round waves, but especially Rhossili Bay to the far west. Lessons on Gower can be booked through Gower Surfing Development. Owner Simon Jayham is known for his big wave surfing exploits, and he or his instructors should have you confidently up on a board in no time. Near Rhossili is the pretty village of Llangennith, home of PJ's Surf Shop. Beginners' lessons take two hours and you can also book one-to-one sessions.

INFO Gower Surfing Development 01792 360370 gowersurfing.com
STAY In Rhossili Bay or nearby Port Eynon 01792 361302 visitmumbles.co.uk

Right: Croyde Bay, Devon

8 For Devon cream

Croyde Bay, Devon

James Cracknell, renowned Olympic oarsman, loves Croyde so much that he named his son after it. It's easy to empathise with his enthusiasm. In strong swells, Croyde can offer some of the fastest waves in England, but it's also a great place to learn to surf. The Point Breaks surf school is fully accredited to the British Surfing Association and prides itself on a high success rate. Oh, and you can have a cream tea in Croyde afterwards. Beginners' lessons are three hours long.

INFO Point Breaks surf school 07776 148679 pointbreaks.com
STAY In Croyde or nearby Saunton Sands 01271 870553 woolacombe tourism.co.uk, or visitdevon.co.uk

9 For an elegant setting

Bigbury-on-Sea, Devon

Bigbury is a stunning place to surf, with Burgh Island and its Art Deco hotel a stone's throw away. The Discovery Surf School is one of the best in the UK, though don't expect big swell in the summer. Owner Martin Connolly is an experienced surfer and lifeguard, having worked several seasons on Australian beaches. The maximum ratio of pupils to instructor is 6:1, so you get plenty of individual attention. Martin also teaches stand-up paddle surfing.

INFO Discovery Surf School 07813 639622 discoverysurf.com
STAY In Bigbury-on-Sea or nearby Thurlestone 01548 853195 kingsbridgeinfo.co.uk, or visitdevon.co.uk

Learning to surf on the Gower Peninsula

10 For stand-up paddle surfing

Tynemouth, Tyne & Wear
Its devotees claim that stand-up paddle surfing is the oldest form of surfing. Ancient Polynesians certainly rode boards with paddles, and now, with the likes of celebs Kate Hudson, Jennifer Aniston and even the former 007 himself, Pierce Brosnan, taking to the sport, it's catching on in the UK.
The immaculate beach at Tynemouth is a great place to give it a go under the expert eye of Joe Thwaites, of local company Boardskillz. By the end of a taster lesson, you'll be ready for the challenge of conventional surfing, too. A taster lesson takes two hours.
INFO Boardskillz 0191 258 1499 boardskillz.co.uk
STAY In Tynemouth or nearby Whitley Bay 0191 200 8535 visitnorthtyneside.com

11 For a swell forecast

Coldingham Bay, Eyemouth, Berwickshire
On a good day, waves as enjoyable as any north of the border draw surfers to this rare sand beach on the rocky

Coldingham Bay, Eyemouth, Berwickshire

east coast. As well as being sheltered, the bay forms part of Scotland's only Voluntary Marine Nature Reserve. St Vedas Surf Shop, in the bay, sells and hires all the gear as well as running a surf school and keeping a beady eye on the waves with two webcams. Check out its website for tide times and a five-day animated swell forecast.
INFO St Vedas Surf Shop 01890 771679 stvedas.co.uk
STAY In Eyemouth or nearby Berwick-upon-Tweed 018907 50678 or 01289 330733 visitnorthumberland.com

12 For a man-made reef

Bournemouth, Dorset
Europe's first artificial surf reef isn't in Cornwall, Devon, Wales or any other of the country's better known hotspots, but just a few hundred metres from Boscombe Pier, Bournemouth. Even prior to its completion, the reef improved wave quality, by shaping the waves which break on or near it and its arrival is an undeniable coup for an area that has long had a dedicated surfing community. After a session or two with Bournemouth Surf School you could watch local experts doing their thing on the man-made surf break.
INFO 07733 895538 bournemouthsurfschool.co.uk
STAY In Bournemouth or nearby Poole 0845 051 1700 bournemouth.co.uk

Snorkelling

While there is a whole world of beautiful and interesting things to explore on the beach and in rockpools, there is something else out there in the sea. With a mask, snorkel and flippers, you can

Ballan Wrassse
Labrus bergylta
DISTINGUISHING MARKS This large, chunky fish has a big mouth and flattened sides to its body, in a variety of spots and colours. Can be very inquisitive and investigates snorkellers from a respectful distance. Up to 50cm.
WHERE TO FIND Widespread in British waters, especially in the north and east.
A CURIOUS THING This fish starts life as a female, and may turn male as it grows older.

Kelp
Laminaria digitata
DISTINGUISHING MARKS There are various kinds of this large seaweed, sometimes with just one blade, or branched into many fingers. Usually olive-green to brown.
WHERE TO FIND All around the UK, forming forests just below the low water mark.
A CURIOUS THING The holdfasts (roots) of kelp often wash up on the beach, looking like skeletal animal parts.

Sea Slug
Coryphella browni
DISTINGUISHING MARKS Although they sound unprepossessing, most are brightly coloured and exquisitely beautiful, and quite unlike their garden relatives. They are 2–3cm in length.
WHERE TO FIND All around our coasts, especially in spring and summer.
A CURIOUS THING You'll often find their eggs laid in a distinctive pattern underneath rocky crags.

experience a totally fascinating underworld in glorious Technicolor, filled with wildlife you might never have seen before. Snorkelling is a great way to build up confidence in the water and it's a good way to get the whole family involved in something together. It's easy to learn – see the British Sub-Aqua Club's website (bsac.com) for information and courses to get you started.

Spiny Seahorse
Hippocampus histrix
DISTINGUISHING MARKS Cute, unmistakable creature. Yellow to green with prominent soft spines. Large for a seahorse, up to 18cm.
WHERE TO FIND Among seagrass on the south coast (rare).
A CURIOUS THING The male seahorse carries eggs and gives birth to live young.

Squat Lobster
Galathea strigosa
DISTINGUISHING MARKS A little like a crab, a lot like a lobster – a few different kinds can be encountered by the keen snorkeller. Up to 10cm long.
WHERE TO FIND Everywhere, close to rocky shelter, in deep pools when the tide is out.
A CURIOUS THING Usually very shy, but can be quite approachable at popular bathing spots where they are accustomed to swimmers.

Sea Bass
Dicentrarchus labrax
DISTINGUISHING MARKS Silver to dark grey, with large scales and a prominent, spiny dorsal fin. Up to 80cm.
WHERE TO FIND In rocky coves and gullies in the south and west.
A CURIOUS THING To the observer, the sea bass is often just a streak of lightning, as it flashes its silvery flank while hunting for small fish in the shallows.

Weekends for adventure sports

Why be stuck inside when you could be cresting a wave on a windsurfer, cantering through the surf on horseback or blasting across the beach with a powerkite? Try a new adventure sport such as coasteering or sea kayaking and you will give yourself a confidence-boosting rush of adrenaline and feelgood endorphins, and you'll also get to see the coast from a different perspective. You need to know what you're doing, so we have tracked down some of the best places with instructors to help you get started.

This page: Land yachting, like traction kiting, is adrenaline-fuelled

1 For traction kiting

Watergate Bay, Cornwall

Kite flying, that age-old childhood pastime, has grown up. Forget memories of kites bobbing gently in the breeze – today's traction powerkites harness the wind's force to blast you across the beach at up to 30 miles an hour, on your feet (skudding), on a landboard (a skateboard with foot straps) or on a buggy (three-wheeled cart). The Extreme Academy is just north of Newquay, and as the beach here is as flat and as straight as a runway, it's a great place for a two-hour lesson, covering safety, reading the wind 'window' and the basics of how kites fly, steer and produce power. Once you get the hang of it, racing across the sand is a real blast. Other sports taught here include surfing, kitesurfing, waveskiing and more.

INFO Extreme Academy 01637 860840 watergatebay.co.uk STAY The Hotel 01637 860543 watergatebay.co.uk, or in nearby Newquay 01872 322900 visitcornwall.com

2 For powerboating

Southampton, Hampshire

Petrol heads can experience life at full throttle behind the wheel of a powerboat. Skimming across the waves with all that force behind you is fun, fast and super-exhilarating. Seven-times world champion Neil Holmes runs a powerboat training school in Southampton, where he can give you a race taster experience, learning how to drive a boat at speed around the same race course on which he teaches national champions. Also on offer is the RYA (Royal Yachting Association) Level 2; this will give you a basic grounding (or should that be waving?) in the skills you'll need to manoeuvre a modest-sized boat. Some of the course is classroom-

Coasteering has leapt in popularity

based to digest all the important gen on safety equipment, navigation and man overboard procedure, but after that you'll have at least two runs out on Southampton Water learning to turn, steer and, perhaps most important of all, stop. An experience to remember.

INFO Neil Holmes Powerboat Training Academy 07900 453305 powerboatcentre.com STAY White Star Tavern 023 8082 1990 whitestartavern.co.uk, or elsewhere in Southampton 023 8083 3333 visit-southampton.co.uk

3 For spearfishing
Portland, Dorset

For an invigorating way to get in touch with the elements and hopefully catch your supper at the same time, have a stab at underwater spearfishing. In its modern guise, it dates back to the 1930s. This is about free-diving (without sub-aqua gear) and hunting the fish using a speargun that fires a bolt. No licence is needed but safety is vital so tuition makes sense.

Beach riding, Pembrokeshire

You'll need some kit: a close-fitting wetsuit, neoprene hood, fins, mask and snorkel – not quite James Bond in *Thunderball* but still pretty cool. A weekend course covers tides, currents, weather conditions and how to shoot safely and there's plenty of time to get out there and have a go. It includes hotel accommodation for Saturday night, and lunch. INFO portlandspearoacademy. co.uk STAY Accommodation included

4 For coasteering
Polzeath, Cornwall

In the past few years, coasteering – working along

a coastal route by any means necessary – has leapt in popularity. You need to be reasonably fit and not averse to getting wet, as you'll end up experiencing the coast in an up close and personal way. On the Introduction course, you'll spend over two hours in the sea, exploring caves, scrambling over rock platforms, swimming across inlets, climbing above deep water and leaping off some exciting ledge jumps (all jumps are optional), with experienced British Coasteering Federation trained instructors. All this takes place in Port Quin – a secluded natural port, relatively sheltered from

Scuba diving, Babbacombe Beach, Torquay, Devon

6 For windsurfing

Brandon Bay, County Kerry

Brandon Bay on the Dingle Peninsula is a paradise for windsurfers. And in Jamie Knox, it's blessed with a man who was once one of the best at the sport on the planet. Knox decamped from the World Tour to set up his windsurfing centre there in 1990, catering for all levels from beginner to professional. Even if you've never managed to master standing up on a windsurfer, Jamie and his team promise to get you up and away in no time. Once you've got the basics you can go on to conquer sailing upwind and have an introduction to improved turning and harness work. A Start Windsurfing course takes two days, and this is also a great area for horse riding, hill walking and cycling.

INFO Jamie Knox Watersports Ireland 00353 66 7139411 jamieknox.com

STAY In Castlegregory and the Maharees or nearby Cloghane 0808 234 2009 discoverireland.com

Right: Coasteering near Polzeath, Cornwall

swell. Intermediate and Advanced courses are also available at Port Gaverne.

INFO Cornish Rock Tors 07791 533569 cornishrocktors.com

STAY Cornish Rock Tors provide a list of suggested accommodation nearby

5 For beach riding

Druidstone Haven beach, near Haverfordwest, Pembrokeshire

There is something irresistibly romantic about riding through the surf on a long stretch of sandy beach. Cantering along, wind whipping the horses' manes – it's the stuff of dreams. Very few beaches in the UK allow horse riding on the sand, but Nolton Stables in Pembrokeshire's Coastal National Park specialises in beach riding, so it is a good place to start. To break you in gently, you can opt for three one-and-a-half-hour rides over two days and will be carefully matched to a suitable steed. Sand makes a great year-round terrain and whether your horse is walking sedately or plunging forward into a canter through the waves, it's an exhilarating experience.

INFO Nolton Stables 01437 710360 noltonstables.com

STAY Nolton Stables can recommend various options, or visitpembrokeshire.com

Sandboarding at Braunton Burrows, Devon

8 For water confidence

Dunroamin Beach, Lake, Isle of Wight

On a beach midway between Shanklin and Sandown, Wight Water Adventure Watersports offers a range of fun and professional training courses but prides itself on its 'water confidence' introduction to watersports. Courses for adults, teens and children are designed as a safe but exciting way to experience the thrill of surfing, sailing and canoeing. Two-hour 'Splash' sessions for the under-16s include kayaking, bodyboarding and beach games, and there is a kids' club for under-15s on Sundays. Adults can join in the fun, too – wetsuits and buoyancy aids are provided. The centre also runs courses in surfing, windsurfing and stand-up paddle surfing, and it hires out canoes, sailing boats, surf boards and so on.
INFO 01983 404987 wightwaters.com
STAY In Shanklin or Sandown, IoW Tourist Information 01983 813813 islandbreaks.co.uk

7 For sandboarding

Braunton Burrows, Devon

There are few sports that allow you to immerse yourself in a great heap of sand dunes and frolic in the sunshine, but sandboarding – basically, like snowboarding onland – is the exception to the rule. If you have already tried surfing, snowboarding or skateboarding, you'll have an advantage, as the principles of balance are the same, but it's a good idea to have a lesson first to see whether you like it before committing to buying your own board. Also, you will be advised on the best way to protect the delicate eco-system of the dunes.

Braunton Burrows in north Devon has some of the highest dunes in the UK and you can take half-day lessons there with an instructor from the Barefoot Surf School. Other popular places to sandboard around the UK include Holywell Bay, near Newquay in Cornwall, Porth Dinllaen Dunes on the Llyn Peninsula and Rhosneigr Dunes in Anglesey. You'll get sandy and sweaty and you'll often end up a heap but it's still a brilliant way to get fit while having no end of fun.
INFO Barefoot Surf School 01271 891231 barefootsurf.com
STAY In Barnstaple or nearby Braunton 01271 375000 staynorthdevon.co.uk

9 For waveskiing

Porthcawl, Mid Glamorgan

A cross between sea kayaking and surfing, waveskiing is a good way to get instant kicks and, as it's still relatively 'niche', is a fun and friendly sport to try. The board is like a light and fairly flexible surfboard that you sit on, with grooves for the seat and footholds to help you balance and stay aboard. It takes a little practice to get the hang of it – you sit on top of it and turn using body movements and a paddle – but instructors say that anyone can take part, regardless of age, skill or fitness and that just one hour's tuition will get you out and paddling. Catching the waves is the next challenge! Kit includes wetsuit, lifejacket and helmet, paddle and board, all of which are provided when you take a lesson. Try a half-day taster course and you could get the bug.
INFO Adventures Outdoor Activity Centre 01656 782300 adventureswales.co.uk
STAY Fairways Hotel 01656 782085 thefairwayshotel.co.uk, or elsewhere in Porthcawl welcometoporthcawl.co.uk

10 For childlike abandon

Oxwich Bay, Gower Peninsula

The majestic Gower Peninsula – the first place in Britain to be designated an Area of Outstanding Natural Beauty – not only offers exquisite scenery and just

Windsurfing, Brandon Bay, County Kerry

about every watersport you can imagine, but it's also a great place to have some pure, unabashed fun – courtesy of a 'ringo' ride at Oxwich Bay. Ringo rides are provided as part of Ocean and Earth's 'wet 'n' wild' activity packages, which also include canyoning and kayaking, and full-board accommodation in dormitory-style rooms. Sit in a donut (an inflatable tyre) and then have the spin of a lifetime around the bay behind a speedboat. The team boat drivers will also reveal what onions are – but be warned, you'll want more. Kids will love it.
INFO 01639 700388
oceanandearth.co.uk
STAY At Merlins Hostel or Oxwich Bay Hotel 01639 700388
oceanandearth.co.uk

11 For scuba diving

Babbacombe Beach, Torquay, Devon
The Gulf Stream provides divers with relatively warm water (18–19°C in late summer) and plenty to see – visibility is more than 15 metres in calm periods. You can get into the water from the shore. Discover colourful jewel anemones, cuttlefish, crabs and lobsters as you explore underwater caves before exchanging stories with fellow divers at the beach café afterwards. Divers Down provides tuition, arranges accompanied or unaccompanied dives and supplies and services a full range of diving equipment, underwater scooters and dive kayaks.
INFO Babbacombe Beach Café and Dive Centre 01803 324532
babbacombebeach.com.
Divers Down 01803 327111
diversdown.co.uk
STAY In Babbacombe or nearby Torquay 0844 474 2233 englishriviera.co.uk

12 For getting wet and wild

Adventure North Wales, Abersoch, Llyn Peninsula
Can't make your mind up which of the many adventure sports to try? If you take a weekend trip with Adventure North Wales to the popular sailing resort of Abersoch, you can try more than one sport in a weekend. How about combining whitewater rafting with canyoning (leaping into rockpools, sliding down rock slabs, riding a zip run over a waterfall)? Or maybe you'd like to try coasteering (climbing, scrambling, cliff jumping and swimming along the rocky coast) and single-seater kayaking? If you need more choice, you might try the 'Awesome 4some' – powerboating, coasteering, donut rides and canyoning. The breaks include accommodation, and you can take your pick from hotel, B&B or self-catering.
INFO Adventure North Wales 0845 365 4265
adventure-northwales.com
STAY Various options – see adventure-northwales.com for details

Right: Stand-up paddle surfing is strenuous but good fun

Weekends for oars and sails

As an island nation, seafaring is a part of our DNA. Whether we are paddling our own canoes, hoisting up the mainsail or just watching from the quay as someone else does it, it seems that we are never happier than when we're out on the ocean waves. All around our shores there are great opportunities to take to the water – either as a novice or a seasoned seasalt – or to join in the fun of a regatta or sailing festival. We've rounded up a selection of the best ways to enjoy our maritime heritage.

This page: Round The Island Race, Isle of Wight

Running the rapids, Findhorn, Forres, Morayshire

1 For dinghy sailing

**Snettisham Beach,
King's Lynn, Norfolk**
Formed in 1937 by a group
of beach bungalow owners
who wanted to race their
craft, Snettisham Beach
Sailing Club continues to
provide dinghy racing on
the sea and an inland lake
for sailing. Snettisham is a
popular venue for Enterprise,
Laser 2000 and Dart 18
Catamarans but, with a
newly refurbished clubhouse
right on the beach, the club
says it caters for all – from
those who want to potter
about in boats to national
champions and 'pretty much
everyone enjoys the bar!'
The sailing season runs
from Easter to October.
INFO Snettisham Beach
Sailing Club 01485 540639
snetbeach.co.uk
STAY In Snettisham or nearby
Hunstanton 01485 532610
visitwestnorfolk.co.uk

2 For 2012 fever

**Portland Harbour,
Portland, Dorset**
Home to the 2012 Olympic
sailing events, Portland
Harbour also offers every
type of watersport, from
kayaking to scuba diving
and windsurfing. One of the
largest man-made harbours
in the world, with three
breakwaters built by the
Royal Navy, it functions as
a fully-fledged commercial
port as well as a Mecca for
watersports enthusiasts.
There is plenty of room for
everyone in the harbour,
which is sheltered from the
prevailing south-westerly
winds by Chesil Beach.
Olympic host Weymouth
& Portland National Sailing
Academy (WPNSA) offers
sailing lessons for all abilities.
INFO Portland Marina
08454 302012

portlandmarina.co.uk.
WPNSA 01305 866000
wpnsa.co.uk
STAY In Weymouth or nearby
Abbotsbury 01305 785747
visitweymouth.co.uk

3 For sheer variety
**Findhorn Bay, Forres,
Morayshire**
Associated with the spiritual
community based a mile
outside this east coast
village, Findhorn is also
a draw for all types of
watersports enthusiasts.
Boatie types head for the
Royal Findhorn Yacht Club
or the Findhorn Marina,
where you can learn dinghy
and powerboat sailing.
Upstream, Ace Adventure
offers introductory courses
in inflatable boats for canoe
and kayak novices keen to
learn how to run the rapids
of the Findhorn River.
Salmon and mackerel fishing
is another option, while the
bay itself is a popular venue
for windsurfing.
INFO Royal Findhorn Yacht
Club 01309 690247
rfyc.net. Findhorn Marina
01309 690099
findhornmarina.com. Ace
Adventure 01479 810510
aceadventures.co.uk

STAY In Findhorn Bay or
nearby Forres 01309 673701
visitscotland.com

4 For serious sailing
**Minnis Bay, Birchington,
Kent**
Described as one of Kent's
best-kept secrets, Minnis
Bay is home to a sailing club,
which makes the most of the
long, sandy beach and calm
waters of the tidal bay.
Although catamaran and
dinghy racing forms the

greater part of the club's
business, it also caters for
year-round cruising.
The club has three fully
operational boats that
members can hire for a
nominal fee and arranges
Royal Yachting Association
sail-training courses.
INFO Minnis Bay Sailing Club
01843 841588
minnisbaysailingclub.co.uk
STAY In Minnis Bay or nearby
Westgate-on-Sea 01843
577577 visitthanet.co.uk

Take to the sea with family and friends

5 For barge enthusiasts

Pin Mill Sailing Club, Ipswich, Suffolk

Every June the full-bellied red sails of Thames barges course down the River Orwell during the Pin Mill Sailing Club Barge Match. Thames barges were the container ships of their day, transporting goods in their flat-bottomed hulls. These vintage examples are kept afloat by a band of enthusiasts who restore and race them – the estuaries of Suffolk and Essex would be a much duller place without them. INFO Pin Mill Sailing Club 01473 780271 pmsc.org.uk STAY In nearby villages or in Ipswich 01473 258070 visit-ipswich or visit-suffolk.org.uk

6 For lovers of sailing regattas

Cowes, Isle of Wight

For eight days in August Cowes is a-flutter with hoisted spinnakers, laughter and champagne. Cowes Week is part of the social calendar and is a heady mix

Left: Ruth, a traditional gaff-rigged sailing ship, based in Penzance

of yacht racing – around 1,000 boats and 8,500 competitors take part in 40 daily races – and parties. Look out for fireworks displays, sailing lessons for beginners and charity fund-raising events. The best vantage point, if you get there early enough, is just below the battlements of the Royal Yacht Squadron – the most exciting place to watch the yachts jostle for prime position at the start line. INFO 01983 295 744 cowesweek.co.uk STAY In Cowes or nearby Bembridge, IoW Tourist Information 01983 813813 islandbreaks.co.uk

7 For fishing historians

Mousehole, Cornwall

Travel back in time for the biennial Sea Salts and Sail maritime festival in Mousehole, held in early July (the next is in 2012). Luggers and gaffers hoist their traditional tan-coloured sails and sail together majestically across the bay, while the harbour bustles with activity. Enjoy herring tastings, crab-pot making sessions and tin smelting

demonstrations. Guided tours and film archives give a flavour of the village's fishing heritage. Just remember that it's pronounced 'Mouzzel' by locals. INFO Sea Salts and Sail 01736 731655 seasalts.co.uk STAY In Mousehole or nearby Newlyn 01736 362207 visitcornwall.com

8 For yacht racing

Isle of Wight

The J P Morgan Asset Management Round The Island Race is the most democratic of yacht races, where amateur sailors jostle with international professionals to circumnavigate the 50-mile course round the Isle of Wight. The race typically attracts around 1,700 boats and around 16,000 sailors, so it's up there with the world's biggest yacht races. It is organised by the Island Sailing Club, takes place in June and has been running since 1931. For spectators, the first boats set off in the morning from Cowes, then at ten-minute intervals. There are plenty of vantage points around the island – head for the Needles or a spot on the south coast.

INFO 01983 296621
roundtheisland.org.uk
STAY In Cowes or nearby
Gurnard, IoW Tourist
Information 01983 813813
islandbreaks.co.uk

9 For sailors with L-plates

Solva, Pembrokeshire
Once out of the sheltered
harbour inlet of Solva, there
are 30 square miles of open
water down to St Brides Bay,
often without another craft
in sight, which makes it a
brilliant place to learn to sail.
Solva was once a thriving port
and is still an active fishing
harbour and is hugely popular
with sailing craft. Royal
Yachting Association (RYA)-
accredited Solva Sailboats
sailing school, set up in 1986,
has a fleet of well-equipped
boats, which set sail from
Trinity Quay. Courses are
taught in keelboats or
dinghies – Level 1 will give
you an introduction to sailing;
Level 2 is for improvers and if
you're already at that level
you can take a Seamanship
Skills course or a Day Sailing,
which will give you an
introduction to cruising.
Powerboat courses are
also available.

INFO Solva Sailboats
01437 720972 solva.net
STAY In Solva or nearby
St David's 01437 720392
stdavidsinfo.org.uk, or
visitpembrokeshire.com

10 For old working boats

Yarmouth, Isle of Wight
The whole town gets on
board for the colourful
Yarmouth Old Gaffers
Festival where traditional
gaff-rigged sailing boats
fill the harbour for a summer
weekend ready to race. It is
usually held in late May or
early June – check website
for date. The gaffers provide
a wonderful spectacle as
they race in the harbour and

Seafair Haven, Milford Haven, Pembrokeshire

they are usually joined by a vintage naval steamboat and HMS *Victory*'s cutter. Ashore there is a packed schedule of events, including fancy dress competitions, steel bands, story-telling and much more. If you've any strength left in your sea legs you can dance the night away on Friday and Saturday, although tickets sell out so you'll need to book ahead. INFO 01983 761704 yarmoutholdgaffersfestival. co.uk
STAY In Yarmouth or nearby Freshwater, IoW Tourist Information 01983 813813 islandbreaks.co.uk

Sailing round Needles Lighthouse, Isle of Wight

11 For 'seafairers' and enthusiasts

Seafair Haven, Milford Haven, Pembrokeshire
Enjoy this biennial July maritime festival for traditional and classic vessels, from sail and oar powered, to vintage motorboats, all afloat in Milford Haven's waterway. Don't miss the Bermudan wooden yachts, forerunners of today's sleek versions, plus tall ships, sailing trawlers, old gaffers and Baltic traders. As well as on-

water flotillas to enjoy, there are shore-side festival entertainments and food, and a grand Parade of Sail – a magnificent spectacle that can be viewed from many vantage points. The action takes place in and around the Haven waterway ports of Dale, Angle, Milford Haven itself, Neyland, Cresswell, Lawrenny and the upper reaches of the Cleddau River.
INFO Seafair Haven seafairhaven.org.uk
STAY In and around Milford Haven 01437 771818 visitpembrokeshire.com

12 For first-timers

Poole Afloat, Poole Quay, Dorset
Held each June, Poole Afloat

is one of the UK's biggest annual boating and watersports events which aims to get everyone out on the water – from small children to mature students and everyone in between. Try your hand at everything from motorboats and sailing yachts to RIBs (rigid inflatable boats) – just turn up, book a time slot and go! On the quayside there's all-day live entertainment plus showings of the latest marine equipment and watersports accessories. See website for date.
INFO Poole Afloat 01784 473377 onthewater.co.uk
STAY In Poole or nearby Bournemouth 01202 253253, pooletourism.com

Weekends for out-of-season treats

When wintry days kick in, the options for coastal days out may appear to diminish, but this is actually a great time to have the place to yourself. Pull up your collar and go in search of scudding clouds and rolling seas, or batten down the hatches in a seaside cottage and listen to the pounding of the waves from the comfort of a fireside armchair. If rain completely stops outdoor play, we've rounded up some excellent indoor attractions to capture your imagination too, from sea life sanctuaries to magic shows.

This page: Well wrapped up for a winter walk in Norfolk

Visitor Centre, Cley Marshes Nature Reserve, Norfolk

1 For seaside vaudeville

Showzam, Blackpool, Lancashire

Held annually during February half-term Showzam is a festival that sets Blackpool abuzz with all the glitzy razzamatazz of circus, magic and new variety acts. Events are a mix of ticketed and free: there's everything from a carnival ball in the Tower Ballroom to cabaret and family shows plus the seriously scary arthouse funfair ride, Carnesky's Ghost Train, on the promenade. Go for tricks, illusions and glittery fun.

INFO Showzam 01253 478222 showzam.co.uk

STAY In Blackpool or nearby Lytham 01253 478222 visitblackpool.com

2 For underwater life

Exploris, County Down

Billed as 'an exploration of the Irish Sea', Exploris aquarium in Portaferry is the ideal place to learn about the wildlife found in the waters off this part of the Northern Irish coast. You may need to brave the weather to see the seals in the Seal Sanctuary, but the Irish Coast Zone allows you to see crabs, cuttlefish and juvenile rays in the dry. Afterwards you can wrap up warm for a walk by Strangford Lough to have a look at the natural habitat of the fish and urchins you see in the museum.

INFO 028 42 728062 exploris.org.uk

STAY In Portaferry or nearby Kircubbin 028 9182 6846 ards-council.gov.uk or 0800 039 7000 discovernorthernireland.com

3 For a gander at geese

Cley Marshes Nature Reserve, Norfolk

Cley's famous marshes can be a surprisingly comfortable place to spot birds nowadays, thanks largely to its award-winning, eco-friendly Visitor Centre where you can sit snugly in the warm, sipping a latte and watching marsh harriers fly past the windows. Outside, there are five hides, which overlook the pools and scrapes. The reed beds are considered to be one of the best spots in the UK to see migrating birds and the rain won't bother them one bit.

INFO 01263 740008 norfolkwildlifetrust.org.uk/naturereserves

STAY In Cley Next the Sea or nearby Blakeney 0871 200 3071 visitnorthnorfolk.com

4 For melancholy reflection

New Romney, Kent

On a bright sunny day, the views of sea, sky and shore on the vast flats of Romney Marsh are spectacular. Under leaden wintry skies what better place to hear what the Victorian poet Matthew Arnold called in his famous poem *Dover Beach*, 'the melancholy, long, withdrawing roar' of the tide on the 'naked shingles of the world'? The Romney Bay House Hotel is a 1920s ten-bed house designed by Sir Clough Williams-Ellis (who also designed Portmeirion, the Welsh seaside village made famous by the television series, *The Prisoner*). It's on a private road and is an atmospheric place to spend a weekend.

INFO New Romney Tourist Information 01303 258594 discoverfolkestone.co.uk, or dymchurchonline.com
STAY Romney Bay House Hotel 01797 364 747 romneybayhousehotel.co.uk

5 For watery winter sunsets

The Sound Café, Cregneash, Isle of Man

Huge tinted windows in this modern, slate-clad and turf-roofed visitor centre and café, perched on a hill on the south-western tip of the Isle of Man, offer a panorama of the sound that separates the isle from the islet of Kitterland and the craggy Calf of Man beyond. Sip your tea and watch the sun sink into the Irish Sea.
INFO Sound Café & Visitor Centre 01624 838123

dsleisureltd.com
STAY In Port Erin or nearby Port St Mary 01624 686766 visitisleofman.com

6 For storm watching

Flying Boat Club, Tresco, Isles of Scilly

Winter breaks in Tresco's beachfront houses won't guarantee you a tan, but you could get the full drama of an Atlantic storm crashing in on the cliffs around Piper's Hole, a cave in the north of the island. The Flying Boat Club, formerly the air station for the UK flying boats that flew against German submarines in WWI, features a dozen waterfront cottages to rent, sleeping six to eight people. There's an on-site holiday club where you can use the indoor swimming

The Aldeburgh Bookshop, Aldeburgh, Suffolk

pool, tennis courts, gym, steam room, Jacuzzi and treatment rooms. Entry to the tropical Abbey Garden is also included.
INFO Flying Boat Club 01720 422849 tresco.co.uk
STAY At Flying Boat Club,

or at The New Inn on Tresco 01720 422844 tresco.co.uk

7 For holing up with a good book
The Aldeburgh Bookshop, Aldeburgh, Suffolk
Entertainment – in the shape of a good book – runs year-

round in Aldeburgh. As well as maps and guides, this much lauded bookshop stocks and sells online literature by local luminaries, such as Ronald Blythe, and publishes its own titles. Its annual Aldeburgh Literary Festival in March has drawn writers as diverse as Doris Lessing and Will Self, and, according to one festival-goer, offers 'bracing sea air, intimacy and intellectual sharpness'.
INFO 01728 452389 aldeburghbookshop.co.uk
STAY In Aldeburgh or nearby Snape Maltings 01728 453637 suffolkcoastal.gov.uk, or thesuffolkcoast.co.uk

8 For a blow along the cliffs
Hell's Mouth, near Portreath, Cornwall
In winter, the north Cornish coast assumes a rugged splendour far removed from its bucket and spade summer alter ego. Walking along the South West Coast Path on a windy day is a reminder of raw elemental power – and man's frailty in the face of it. Many ships have been wrecked in the

Exploris aquarium, Portaferry, County Down

aptly named Hell's Mouth, a churning, rocky chasm filled with a deafening tumult of sea and spume. INFO southwestcoastpath.com

STAY In Portreath or neaby Porthtowan 01209 219048 visitcornwall.com

9 For boys' toys

The Helicoptor Museum, Weston-super-Mare, Somerset

A short drive or bus ride from Weston-super-Mare's Grand Pier, this unique museum houses the world's largest collection of helicopters, including a Russian gunship with four missile launchers, two aircraft of The Queen's Royal Flight and veterans of the Vietnam conflict. In winter, Air Experience flights of about seven minutes long, go up on one Sunday a month, taking you for a flight out over the bay with fine views of the coastline and the pier. Call ahead to check dates.

INFO 01934 635227 helicoptermuseum.co.uk

STAY In Weston-super-Mare or nearby Clevedon 01934 888800 visitsomerset.co.uk

10 For sheer eccentricity

Under the Pier Show, Southwold, Suffolk

The marvellous, coast Award-winning Southwold

Otters at the Scottish Sea Life Sanctuary, Oban, Argyll

Pier is the perfect setting for this paean to British eccentricity and wit. Artist and inventor Tim Hunkin has re-imagined the typical amusement arcade and come up with attractions that intrigue, amuse and confound. Try the Microbreak holiday simulator, the Quickfit exercise machine or take a virtual dog on a walk and watch it get into virtual scraps. The Quantum Tunnelling Telescope 'focuses time and space to bring you everything you could possibly want to see through a pier telesccope'. Very much a place to loosen the imagination, for children and adults alike.

INFO 01502 722105, underthepier.com and southwoldpier.co.uk

STAY In Southwold or nearby Walberswick 01502 724729 visit-southwold.co.uk or visit-sunrisecoast.co.uk

11 For cute creatures
Scottish Sea Life Sanctuary, Oban, Argyll

With rescued seals and otters abounding, this sea life sanctuary is very much the place to go to coo over seals up close. Set on the shores of Loch Creran, it also has an aquarium housing sharks, stingrays and starfish. Almost all the sea creatures featured here can be found in the lochs of the west Highlands or in the nearby Atlantic. There is even a seahorse stud farm on site, to help ease the pressure on wild stocks. And if you should become especially attached in any way, you can sign up for the seal pup adoption scheme.

INFO 01631 720386 sealsanctuary.co.uk

STAY Oban Tourist Information 01631 563122 visitscotland.com, or visitscottishheartlands.com

12 For a long view
Spinnaker Tower, Portsmouth, Hampshire

Portsmouth's millennium project opened five years after the main event, but the 170-metre-high Spinnaker Tower more than makes up for the wait with its views. Its sail-like structure has a crow's nest viewing platform at its apex, which allows you to see for up to 23 miles. This panorama may be more restricted if you happen to be there in driving rain – or even a snowstorm – but you can still get a great look in and around the harbour and coastline from its three viewing decks.

INFO 023 9285 7520 spinnakertower.co.uk

STAY In Portsmouth or nearby Southsea 023 9282 6722 visitportsmouth.co.uk

Right: The Under the Pier Show, Southwold, Suffolk

Hell's Mouth, near Portreath, Cornwall

This page: (Not) sharing a lolly at Weston-super-Mare, Somerset

Index

Picture credits

161 © Corbis. All Rights Reserved.
162 © PulpFoto/Alamy
163 © Mark Bolton
Photography/Alamy
164 © Daniel Start
165 © Country Living Magazine
167 © Simon Dack/Alamy
168/169 © Justin Walker/ZEST
Magazine
170 © Bob Berry/VisitCornwall Photo
Gallery
171 © Charlie Jay/Sennen Surfing
Centre
172 © NowRf/Alamy
173 ©Anne Harriott
2009/www.pointbreaks.com
174 © www.surfgsd.com
175 © Dougie Wilson/St Vedas Surf
Shop
176/177 Illustrations/Mike
Langman/coast Magazine
178/179 © Buzz Pictures/Alamy
180 © Emma Scattergood/coast
Magazine
181 © Anthony Crolla/coast
Magazine
182 © Terry Griffiths
183 © Mike
Newman/www.CornishRockTors.com
184 © Nicola Smith/coast Magazine
185 © Jamie Knox Watersports
187 © www.star-board-sup.com
188/189 © Patrick Eden
190 © Ace Adventure – The White
Water Rafting Specialists/
www.AceAdventures.co.uk
191 ©Charles Roff/Country Living
Magazine
192 © Andrew Montgomery/coast
Magazine/used by permission of
www.firstratesail.co.uk

194 ©John Arcus/Seafair Haven
Festival
195 © Ginny Goodman/Alamy
196/197 Copyright 2010
photolibrary.com
198 © Richard Osbourne/Norfolk
Wildlife Trust
199 ©The Aldeburgh Bookshop
200 © Paul Kay/Exploris
201 © The Scottish SEALIFE Sanctuary
202 © Mike Greenslade/Alamy
203 © Tim Hunkin/The Under the Pier
Show
204 © Adrian Sherratt/Alamy

Acknowledgements

Grateful thanks go to coast Magazine's valued contributors for their help in seeking out our **250 weekends by the sea**:
Iain Aitch; Alf Aldersen; Sharon Amos; Linda Bird; Allan Brodie; Laura Dixon; Andrew Eames; Sarah Evans; Eddi Fiegel;
Joanne Finney; Clare Gogerty; Michele, Joe and Louis Jameson; Stuart Kirby; Kate Langrish; Jonathan Lee; Sian Lye;
Elizabeth Mahoney; Paula McWaters; Claire Norton; Rachael Oakden; Mary-Vere Parr; Rufus Purdey; Amy Raphael;
Alex Reece; Caroline Reeds; Nicola Smith; Mat Snow; Christopher Somerville; Paul Stokes; Sian Thatcher;
Adrian Tierney-Jones; Alex Wade; Alison Walker; Ali Watkinson; Susie Wood; Jonny Young.
Shore spotter's guides: words/Richard Harrington; illustrations/Mike Langman, Richard Woodgate.